BUSINESS AND ACADEMIA

BUSINESS AND ACADEMIA

PARTNERS IN NEW ENGLAND'S ECONOMIC RENEWAL

Editors:
John C. Hoy
Melvin H. Bernstein

A Futures of New England Book
Published for New England Board of Higher Education by
UNIVERSITY PRESS OF NEW ENGLAND
Hanover and London, 1981

UNIVERSITY PRESS OF NEW ENGLAND

Brandeis University
Brown University
Clark University
Dartmouth College
University of New Hampshire
University of Rhode Island
Tufts University
University of Vermont

Library of Congress Catalogue Card Number 80–54467
International Standard Book Number 0–87451–197–6
Printed in the United States of America
Library of Congress Cataloguing in Publication data will be found on the last printed page of this book.

CONTENTS

PREFACE

This book, a first step toward a new literature on the relationship of higher education to the health of the economy, provides a rationale for change in some of the attitudes and policies within the higher-education community of New England which have prevailed during its 1945–75 period of prosperity and growth. From 1976 to 1980 the pattern nationally and in this region shifted to a steady state and the formalization of no-growth policies. The unique fact of New England as the birthplace of public education and higher education in America gives special significance to the region's problems and opportunities in the 1980s.

The impetus for the book was a comprehensive examination by the Commission on Higher Education and the Economy of New England of the special role of colleges and universities in fostering the long-term prosperity of the New England economy. The Commission, established by the New England Board of Higher Education, is composed of thirty-one distinguished New England representatives of business, government, academia, and labor. Research papers on issues confronting the Commission were presented by scholars and public policy commentators at a Hartford, Connecticut, conference on December 16, 1980.

The cluster of papers that led to the development of this book defined the role of higher education in the planning and implementation of regional economic policy. Of special interest to the Commission is the refinement and definition of specific ways in which the region's colleges and universities can act collectively to contribute to economic prosperity.

Two central issues which the Commission decided to consider, and which are addressed in the following pages, are:

Why should institutions of higher education want to help the economy of the region?

What can these institutions do to assist the economy of the region?

In addition, the Commission is concerned about the interface between academia and both private industry and government. The interface involves perceptions and attitudes of each sector which, we realize, can from time to time dominate the effectiveness of the cooperative process. Thus a full understanding of the positive and negative aspects of current and established relations is important.

In assessing the prospective contributions of colleges and universities to the economic development of New England, the Commission is interested in an overview and analysis of academic contributions in other regions. The assumption is that much can be learned from their experience.

Finally, the book furthers the Commission's goal of providing research information in four other areas:

A review, with documentation, of the contributions that higher educational institutions have already made.

A precise definition of the economic and social dimensions of the anticipated industrial mix of the early 1980s and its implications for institutions of higher education.

A documentation of current institutional strengths that are relevant to economic development in the regional economy, and how institutions may influence that development.

Identification, from the lessons and experiences of the 1945–75 period, of aspects relevant to new problems confronting state and regional economic policymakers and the ways in which institutions of higher education may address them.

The statements of Ray Stata and Russell Brace in Appendix II reveal the perspective of two business leaders on the issues examined in this book. Their thoughtful views reflect well the appreciation of the private sector for the linkage needed today between higher education and both business and government.

I strongly believe the collective wisdom found in the following pages expands our understanding of the important role that higher education can play in furthering economic development in New England.

John C. Hoy, *President*
New England Board of Higher Education

ACKNOWLEDGMENTS

We are grateful to the distinguished foundations that have supported the first stage of the work of the Commission and made this book possible. The Ford Foundation through Fred E. Crossland, Program Officer, provided the seed money to launch the Commission project. The W. K. Kellogg Foundation through Arlon E. Elser, Program Director, and the Andrew Mellon Foundation through Clair List, Program Director, provided grants to support the studies, writing, conferences, and publications that define the issues and needs of the New England economy and higher education. The Calvin K. Kazanjian Economics Foundation through John C. Schramm, Managing Director, provided a gift to continue the analysis of New England's economic needs and to publish the findings.

There is little precedent for a project promoting the regional relationship and reciprocal interaction of higher education with private industry. The vision of the foundations supporting the project of the New England Board and its Commission has made possible the dissemination of new data, information, and ideas found in the chapters of this book.

We are also indebted to the Corporate Council members who have given gifts supporting the work of the Commission. The leadership exhibited by these corporations has given the Commission latitude in shaping its investigations to timely economic issues confronted in New England. The founding members of the Corporate Council include:

The Barnes Group Inc.
The Continental Group Inc.
The Digital Equipment Corporation
The First National Bank of Boston
General Electric Foundation
Germanium Power Devices Corporation
The Hartford Insurance Group
The Raytheon Company
The Rogers Corporation
Wheelabrator Frye Inc.

Finally, the editors wish to express their appreciation to Donna Humphrey for her skillful administrative assistance under sometimes hectic conditions and to Barbara Pierpoint for her untiring and efficient secretarial support.

John C. Hoy
Melvin H. Bernstein

Wenham, Mass.
June 1980

BUSINESS

AND ACADEMIA

1. EMERGING NEEDS OF A REINDUSTRIALIZED ECONOMY

Melvin H. Bernstein

Led by high-technology industries, New England came through the 1980 national recession in better condition than at any time since World War II. Rebounding from the 1974–75 recession, the economy improved until 1978, when the region's unemployment rate dipped below the national level for the first time in the decade and has remained below it ever since. At the end of 1980, unemployment in New England was nearly two points under the national average of 7.4 percent. "The transition from textiles and shoes to high tech lines—computers, instruments, electronic equipment, aircraft—appears to be largely complete," says Lynn E. Browne of the Federal Reserve Bank.[1]

The replacement of textile and leather operations with high-technology business caused great economic hardship in New England, but now that the process is virtually ended, some of the resulting benefits can readily be seen. High-technology companies moved in to occupy more than 200 million square feet of floor space formerly occupied by textile and apparel companies. Raytheon houses a major operation in the large American Woolen Company Mill in Shawsheen, Massachusetts. Digital Equipment began its operations in the old Maynard, Massachusetts, plant of American Woolen. Sanders Associates took over one million square feet of space formerly occupied by the Nashua Manufacturing Company in New Hampshire.

As the nation moves toward reindustrialization in the 1980s, New England's post World War II economic experience suggests future directions to be taken. Writing in 1966, R.C. Estall, a British economist analyzing New England's economic condition, concluded, "It is perhaps not fanciful to foresee this region, true to its past, blazing a trail of readjustment for later comers to follow with assurance."[2] New England's growing reputation for having accomplished the shift from obsolescent industries to advanced technology was acknowledged by *Time* Magazine when it recognized that "New England has already achieved the reindustrialization that is the goal" of the nation. "New England first suffered the symptoms of economic decay, depression, and disillusionment that have now become so common in American business. In place of its once mighty, but now outmoded, industries, the region has built a new economic base primarily on high-technology companies."[3] In a speech in Portland, Maine, in 1980, Alexander B. Trowbridge, president of the National Association of Manufacturers, spoke of New England's sparking the American Industrial Revolution, and now leading the revitalization of America's lagging economy. "Research, development, innovation and other technological aspects of productivity have played a big part in the economic rebirth of New England," he said.[4]

In 1951 the Committee on the New England Economy of the President's Council of Economic Advisers defined the "New England Economic Problem."[5] The paramount issue was how to make the most of the region's human and natural resources, including the resource of ideas, in facilitating the adaptation of the industrial structure to changes in New England's underlying competitive position. This issue was not peculiar to New England, nor was it a new problem. The problem was basically one of adapting manufacturing industries, particularly textiles and shoes, to changing technologies and new products and diverting capital resources into newer and expanding industries which emphasize a high ratio of value added to value shipped.

The scientific research base of New England's universities and the business innovations of her graduates have been integral to the economic resurgence of the region. Yet difficult days lie ahead. Competition with the sunbelt and mountain states for high-technology personnel and business is likely to intensify in the decade ahead. Whether New England's colleges and universities can produce the numbers of graduates required in the right mix for advanced technology remains to be seen. Seymour E. Harris, a Harvard economist who co-authored the 1951 study on *The New England Economy* for the President's Council of Economic Advisors, wrote in his own book the following year:

> Many of her major institutions are national in outlook and hence they do not interest themselves in regional problems of research, management and the like. Institutions of higher learning in other regions, particularly in the South and West, contribute much more to the economic development of their regions.[6]

In postindustrial New England the issue is no longer one of shifting from an obsolete industrial base to newer technologies. The issue is to match a sufficiently qualified labor force with the needs of the region's rapidly growing technological industries. The research findings presented in this book indicate both the problems and opportunities the New England states collectively have to address. Leadership survey responses from the public and private sectors further pinpoint definition of the issues and avenues to be taken.

THE IMPACT OF HIGHER EDUCATION ON THE ECONOMY

Charles Stokes finds one clear message emerging from his comparative research on university economic effects in North Carolina, California, Colorado, Michigan, and Illinois. "It is that whether a university or college makes it an act of explicit policy or not, there is such an interaction, a relationship that can readily be traced between what the university community does or does not do and the pace of regional economic development." Even when there is no explicit university leadership, that interaction can be highly effective as in Palo Alto, Boulder-Denver, and Ann Arbor.

After analyzing research and development activities of New England's institutions of higher learning, Peter Doeringer concludes: "that universities are a tremendous technological resource cannot be denied. Further, it may well be that this resource is not being fully utilized. For example, there is evidence to show that many university faculty, varying between 49 percent and 70 percent of those interviewed, have what they think are commercially exploitable ideas. If true, even in part, this may be a potentially huge untapped resource."

Ward Curran's analysis of the resources and expenditures of colleges and universities as a component of state and regional gross product shows that higher education is a vital factor in the economic renaissance of New England. He concludes that it is in the mutual self-interest of government, business, and labor to cooperate jointly with higher education to help promote economic development.

The New England leadership survey on higher education and the economy, reported in Appendix I, indicates that higher education is an underutilized resource in the region's economy. Responding to the survey, the chairman of the board and chief executive of a national corporation with headquarters in Connecticut wrote, regarding the role of New England's colleges and universities:

> In addition to the education-training functions and scientific-technical research work which they are now performing very well, the region's colleges and universities can play a unique role in performing research and in communicating

their findings in such areas as: (1) the impact of federal policies on the region's economy with specific attention to regional income transfer effects; (2) assessing economic problems and potentials; (3) identifying and evaluating existing organizational frameworks, public and private, which affect the region's private leadership.[7]

A view from an official of the executive branch of state government also emphasizes the private sector in commenting on the role of higher education in economic development:

a. Focus research capabilities on developmental problems facing the region.
b. Organize curriculum development efforts to be flexible and readily responsive to changing technology, changing employment trends, and changing economic conditions.
c. As a result of close liaison with private industry and in response to forecasts of employment trends, institutions of higher education should be responsible for (1) informing potential students of changes in future employment conditions, and (2) promoting courses of study which are responsive to those changes.[8]

MANPOWER REQUIREMENTS

New England's chief natural resource is human talent. It always has been from the time the Pilgrims arrived in 1620. Alexis de Tocqueville wrote in *Democracy in America* that "only intellectual power could command influence" among the immigrants who first settled on the New England coast. Nearly four centuries later, as economic issues have moved to the forefront of public concerns for the region and the nation, broadening the base of brainpower in a technology-driven society is seen as the key of the region's future prosperity. Robert Eisenmenger, Director of Research at the Federal Reserve Bank of Boston, has said, "The only comparative economic advantage of New England is that nearly all of its industries are high skill labor-intensive depending on high quality labor which exists in the region."[9]

The problem is that even as New England's colleges and universities prepare to deliver a greater number of technically trained graduates, the growth rate of high-technology industries has created a need for more engineers and computer scientists than can be supplied. This phenomenon, however, is not peculiar to New England. A searching analysis of the national technology manpower shortage by Eva C. Galambos provides these findings:

The nationally recognized Deutsch, Shea, and Evans *High Technology Recruitment Index* reached its highest point in 1979 since 1966, and continues to rise.[10]

Even with increased enrollments, national demand will exceed supply for engineers, computer specialists and other high technology manpower. In the decade of the 1970s, undergraduate engineering enrollment as a percentage of all undergraduate enrollment dipped to a low in 1973, has been rising each year since and reached a high in 1979.

Though the absolute number of college students graduating in high technology fields has been increasing in recent years, the proportion of such baccalaureate degrees to all baccalaureate degrees has declined since 1963–64. The number of engineering baccalaureates in 1979 had finally matched the peak level of 1950 but proportionately the number of such degrees had declined relative to all baccalaureates.

The opportunity to rapidly expand high technology manpower depends largely on the number of high school students who take enough courses in mathematics to begin quantitative curricula when they enter college. That number declined in the 1970s and only recently has begun to turn the corner. At the same time a shortage of mathematics teachers, nationally and regionally, currently exists for school districts, limiting mathematics teaching capability in secondary schools.

Internal academic restraints make it difficult for colleges and universities to shift resources to high demand departments, restricting their ability to adjust quickly to changing market conditions.[11]

In view of the limitations on rapidly expanding the number of graduates in such high-technology fields as computer science, mathematics, engineering, and physical sciences, the demand-supply gap should continue for several years.

In addition to shifting departmental funds and counseling qualified students to major in these fields, another step to alleviate the shortage would be to attract nontraditional students into hard-science majors. Typically, the college-age white male has been the traditional major in mathematics and related technology fields. For example, in 1978 only 3 percent of the nation's engineers were women and one percent black. Overall only 5.5 percent of engineers were members of a minority group. Since the region faces a sharp drop of college-age students in the 1980s, it is both equitable and practical economics to encourage broader participation of women and minorities in technology course programs to prepare for higher paying jobs.

Peter Doeringer's research on labor market conditions in New England shows that student career choices and ultimately educational projections depend on such shifting factors as employment prospects and financial assistance. The important comparisons involve supply and demand not only in the regional labor market but in the country at large. Therefore the labor pool of educated applicants available to New England can be adjusted by enrollment changes or by changing the share of the national supply that is recruited by employers in the region.

Doeringer finds that New England's market share of engineers will decline slightly in the 1980s. The New England share of computer specialists will remain roughly stable. For "engineers and scientists the shortages of the late 1970s will reach into the 1980s. Barring some major shift in demand, balanced labor markets are likely to be achieved in New England, but not until the late 1980s." As for the responsiveness of higher education, he contends that "the current decade is too short a period to accomplish more than quick-fit improvements in the system."

Neal Peirce correctly observes that "manpower need forecasts are vital not just in the high-technology field, but also for the bulk of New England colleges educating native New Englanders for jobs in a broad array of fields." While many colleges have been remiss in understanding and responding to market needs, it is also true that few state or local governments adequately predict future manpower needs. Nor has the business sector fully and consistently articulated its manpower requirements. Pierce concludes that New England's universities and research institutions can make a significant contribution by taking detailed U.S. Department of Labor manpower-demand projections and refining them for regional needs or developing projections on their own.

LEVEL OF COMMUNICATION BETWEEN HIGHER EDUCATION AND BUSINESS, GOVERNMENT, AND LABOR

A huge majority of New England leaders who responded to our survey (Appendix I) felt that although they had some contact with representatives of higher education, communication was not systematic, meaningful, policy-oriented, or significant. In particular, many business leaders and legislators criticized the absence or the nominal character of communication between their sectors and higher education. Nearly four out of five respondents in the survey who commented on the question, and most did, felt that communication was lacking. A few representative opinions will be instructive on how communication between the campuses and private industry or government can be improved. The chairman of the board and chief executive officer of a corporation in New Hampshire:

> I do not recall ever being called from anyone in education asking to talk about what my company is doing and what it expects to need in the way of educated people in the future. A few of us here because of work on boards of overseers with colleges have made some input to the institutions with which we work but there is no concerted effort, that I am aware of, that brings educators and businessmen together to talk about future needs of business and industry, and changes within the institutions themselves. I sense each of us are working somewhat in a vacuum.

The president of a corporation in Connecticut:

> I have the feeling that most colleges and universities feel somewhat above the industrial community—aloof. I believe there needs to be a greater understanding on the part of educators about the market for their product.

The chairman of the board and chief executive officer of a corporation in Rhode Island:

> I think there is a fair amount of superficial communication but my gut feeling is there is not enough down to earth discussion and understanding.

The director of a policy-research university institute in Massachusetts:

> There is a great deal of talk between the sectors and very little communication.

Since there is a widely shared belief among New England leaders that higher education is very important to the regional economy, the issue of communication must be addressed directly if New England is to mobilize its educational resources effectively. Frequently appearing recommendations include:

Agree on ways of obtaining mutually acceptable facts on market needs.

Place less emphasis on "talk" sessions and more on meetings to resolve problems mutually.

Meet at the policy-formation level as well as at the operational level.

Encourage more fixed dialogue rather than ad hoc good-will sessions.

Consult private industry on development of the curriculum. The needs are mutual and changing.

Focus attention of students, faculty, and administrators on the value of the regional economic marketplace, its activities and problems. Student participation in such industry meetings as those of the New England Council, Small Business Association of New England, and Chambers of Commerce would be useful.[12]

Robert McGarrah's case for regional institutes on the campuses is one specific vehicle for engaging students and faculty on research beneficial to the economy of New England. To some extent these institutes exist at many colleges and universities but few have a regional focus. He argues for consolidating "specialized, field research and educational activities into a single institute for regional development contract services." Government and labor as well as business could benefit from such institutes.

STRENGTHENING THE REGIONAL ECONOMY

The higher education and the economy survey reveals a strong commitment by governors and legislators to improve the business climate of their respective states. They recognize the need for attracting new business, keeping existing business, reforming tax systems, expanding technical education and training, and easing the burden of government regulation and red tape. However, a 1980 study of the 48 contiguous American states shows that the three southern New England states had lower business-climate rankings than the three northern tier states.[13]

It is disturbing that while all New England state governments have mounted strong economic development programs, only New Hampshire's reflects the progress made. Changes to improve the business climate apparently have not yet been recognized by manufacturers in five of the six states. These scores suggest either that the changes made in these five states have not taken hold yet or that additional steps must be taken to convince the manufacturers of progress being made.

In the Northeast, three states—Pennsylvania, New York, and New Jersey—had lower rankings than all of the New England states except Connecticut. The greatest competition for New England's growth industries, however, is coming from such sunbelt states as California,

Texas, Colorado, North Carolina, and Florida. Telling comments for the New England leadership survey from the chairman of the board and chief executive officer of a national corporation with headquarters in Massachusetts indicate a volatile situation. Ranking the region's colleges and universities "poor" in helping to meet the labor-force needs of private industry, he said, "Compare the output of engineers and scientists from New England schools with the high technology needs of New England and then look at similar situations in California and Texas." This business executive expects his corporation to remain in New England for the forseeable future but will *expand* outside of New England. He explained, "We will not move existing operations out but will limit expansion due to high tax policies of the Massachusetts legislature and passive attitudes of Rhode Island and Connecticut."

If higher education is to meet its responsibilities for providing highly skilled manpower for private industry in the region, it must protect its share of the student market in a decade of declining enrollments. Neal Peirce suggests several ways this might be accomplished. Essentially he calls for intense joint promotion nationally, listing the rich job opportunities, present and about to open up, for college graduates in the six states. "I would think of a pamphlet which would highlight New England's position as an historically preeminent center of higher education, list the vast array of attractions here, from mountains and seashore to museums, galleries, theaters, and night life, and then contain a capsule paragraph on every college and university of the region."

Finally, on the subject of small business development and venture capital, we know that growth in employment results from the birth and expansion of small firms. Relocation of large firms from one region to another during the past decade has not been a major factor in total business activity and employment of regions. Since New England's economic future has been so closely linked to new business innovation, the availability of venture capital is a critical factor.

Though Boston is a national financial center in the class of New York, Chicago, San Francisco, and Los Angeles, its efforts on behalf of new business in New England have been lackluster. The New England Regional Commission reports that only 40 to 50 percent of financing available through Boston's venture capital corporations is invested in New England; the rest is *exported.* The conservative nature of Boston's venture capitalists is indicated by the fact that only 15 to 20 percent of such capital is invested in start-up firms, compared to California's 25 to

30 percent. In view of present competitive conditions and technological business talent present in New England, economic development requires that greater risks be taken with venture capital available in this region for new firms.

The region's opportunities for economic growth and stability in the 1980s depend on businesses relying heavily on brain power, emerging businesses that may not even have existed a decade ago, and effective marketing of quality products made in New England. Higher education must also market its colleges and universities to bring in students and aggressively identify its services in research and training to private industry. In the words of Maine's former Senate Majority Leader,

> Tough as it is, New England's chances for success at least partially depend on a regional *mentality*. 6 state promotion. 6 state coalition. The intelligent marketing of goods "from New England" requires government involvement.
> We don't have the best climate in the world. We are isolated in the upper right-hand corner of the United States
> But
> to the extent we develop our brainpower, are hardworking and productive—we shall overcome.[14]

To this statement I would add that pursuit of mutual self-interest can only help to preserve resources and enlarge opportunities in New England.

Business Climate Rankings of New England States

State	National Rank 1980	National Rank 1979
New Hampshire	9	21
Maine	24	15
Vermont	27	23
Rhode Island	43	34
Massachusetts	38	37
Connecticut	47	38

2. AN ECONOMIC CONTEXT FOR HIGHER EDUCATION

John C. Hoy

Judging by size alone, higher education is one of the most important industries in New England. Yet higher education is rarely viewed as an industry that vigorously contributes directly and indirectly to the economic health of the region. Usually the tendency is to take higher education for granted as an established resource, one in which budgeted or contributed funds are provided for worthy but intangible purposes. To the contrary, the expenditures of higher education have an immediate and positive effect on the health of New England's economy. In the 1980s, New England will require a strong system of higher education, just as it must develop a healthier and more resilient economy.

The significance of higher education as an economic asset of New England can be readily seen from a few indicators:

Annual expenditures of the 260 colleges and universities in New England in 1980–81 approximate $4 billion and generate an estimated $10 billion, which is about 8 percent of the gross regional product.

Higher education is one of New England's leading "export service" industries, attracting monies into the region from out-of-state students, visitors, corporations, and the federal government.

New England's heavy concentration of outstanding research universities is a major factor in locating new companies here, as well as in retaining existing companies.

New England's 260 institutions of higher learning represent 9 percent of the nation's total of 3,163, even though the region's population represents only 6 percent of all Americans.

Approximately 738,000 full-time students are enrolled in New England's institutions of higher learning: 6 percent of the region's population of 12,500,000.

New England has 50 percent more institutions of higher education per capita than the nation as a whole, and nearly twice as many private institutions per capita as the nation.

New England's proportion of students enrolled in private institutions of higher education is the highest of any region in the nation at 49 percent. Nationally, only 22 percent of college students are enrolled in private higher education.[1]

No accounting of the billions of dollars generated by higher education in the New England economy can measure its real value to the region. Ever since the creation of Harvard College in 1636, New England has benefited from the finest concentration of private institutions of higher learning in the nation. The cultural and learning environment created by these institutions has acted as a magnet to attract and keep in the area many of the best minds in the country: student, graduate, and professor. In the post–World War II period, the collectivity of New England's private colleges and universities has been enhanced by the development of a complementary public system of higher education.

While shrinking resources relative to the surging costs of our inflationary economy imperil New England's institutions of higher learning, perhaps the greatest danger to their continued financial viability is the sharp decrease projected for the pool of high school graduates in this region in the 1980s and early 1990s. A 1979 report of the Western Interstate Commission for Higher Education projected a 16 percent decline in the nationwide pool of high school graduates by 1987 and a 26 percent decline by 1991 (Table 1). Comparative projections for New England are 19 percent by 1987 and 35 percent by 1991. Moreover, while the national downward trend of high school graduates reverses itself between 1991 and 1995, New England shows a continued drop in the pool of high school graduates amounting to 2 percent in the same four-year period and an overall decline of 37 percent since 1979. Fred E. Crossland, the Ford Foundation's program officer for higher education, reported in a 1980 speech at the annual meeting of the Association of Independent Colleges and Universities in Massachusetts that the *actual* contraction of enrollment in the northeastern part of the nation will likely be about 30 percent, twice the national rate of 15 percent.[2] The hardest hit states in New England are expected to be Connecticut, Massachusetts, and Rhode Island. This under-supply will create serious problems for most of the region's colleges and universities; less apparent now but nonetheless real is the secondary impact of the decline on New England business and economic development—losses that will ensue

TABLE 1. Projected Pool of Public High School Graduates in the United States, in New England, and in Each New England State from 1979 to 1995 (percentage of change from 1979)

	1979	1987	1991	1995
U.S.	2,844,871	2,376,722 -16%	2,130,812 -26%	2,279,201 -22%
N.E.	163,689	132,488 -19%	106,596 -35%	103,551 -37%
Conn.	39,051	30,529 -22%	23,554 -40%	22,845 -41%
Me.	15,603	13,571 -13%	12,306 -21%	12,715 -19%
Mass.	78,769	63,013 -20%	48,865 -38%	45,889 -42%
N.H.	11,807	11,108 -6%	10,051 -15%	10,512 -11%
R.I.	11,592	8,447 -27%	6,760 -42%	6,396 -45%
Vt.	6,867	5,820 -15%	5,060 -26%	5,194 -24%

Source: High School Graduates: Projections for the Fifty States, Western Interstate Commission for Higher Education, Boulder, Colo., 1979.

from the diminished manpower pool and income flow caused by fewer graduates.

The region's colleges and universities are naturally concerned with the effect of the anticipated decline on their budgets but have given minimal attention to its effect on the knowledge-intensive labor market, nor have government policymakers been much more aware. Continuing-education programs are not expected to help the diminishing supply of educated labor. Business, understandably, is more alert to the future manpower shortage and has through its industry associations gained increased recognition of the issue within corporate circles.

The student supply problem was well defined by Lynn E. Browne, assistant vice president and economist of the Federal Reserve Bank of Boston, in remarks in June 1980 to the New England Economic Project:

> This is more than a sectoral problem. Our colleges and universities are major employers.... Moreover, the existence of these universities and colleges is probably one of the region's most important locational advantages. The concentration of such institutions attracts young people into the region and increases the supply of professional and technical workers over what it would otherwise be. The presence of the universities creates an intellectual environment which professionals find attractive. If this educational structure were seriously impaired by the problem it will face in the 1980s, industry will pay the price in the following decades.

It is well understood that the future welfare of public colleges and universities is inextricably linked to the health of the New England economy. Government revenues largely fund the budgets of these institutions, and these revenues are derived from taxes which in turn are dependent on the level of economic productivity of each of the six states. But do private institutions of higher learning rise or decline according to the economic health of New England? The region's private colleges and universities do not exist in a vacuum. Many of their contributions come from New England-based corporations and firms. Their tax-exempt status is provided by state government. State scholarships are provided to their students. Faculty and staff pay taxes and benefit from public services. Although the interaction between private education and the region cannot be measured in dollars, a significant relationship exists. Great private institutions like Harvard University, Yale University, and the Massachusetts Institute of Technology clearly have national and international responsibilities, but even for them the regional dimension is of no small consequence.

The problem, then, is twofold: First, how can higher education be strengthened to withstand the shock of sharply decreased enrollments in a period of escalating costs? And, second, how can the higher education resource best be used to contribute to New England's economic development? Three areas deserve special comment: regional economic development, manpower planning, and state funding of higher education. Each of these three critical areas is strongly related to the welfare, responsibilities, and needs of the region's institutions of higher learning.

ECONOMIC DEVELOPMENT

The New England economy that has emerged at the outset of the 1980s bears witness to the successful restructuring that has taken place.

While these changes have occurred, per capita personal income for New Englanders at $8,910 in 1979 was ahead of the U.S. level of $8,773, and the ratio is comparable to that of 1950.[3] The region remains ahead of the nation also in the level of educational attainment of its residents, as well as in the percentage of total population employed in the labor force. New England's competitive edge in research and development, new products development and processes, and innovations in technology is borne out by several illustrations of the size of cutting-edge industries in the region relative to the nation as a whole. With less than 6 percent of the national work force, New England has:

16 percent of U.S. employment in computers

14 percent of U.S. employment in instruments

12 percent of U.S. employment in transportation equipment other than automobiles

10 percent of U.S. employment in electric and electronic equipment.[4]

New England's surprising economic recovery during the last five years raises the question how best in the 1980s to sustain growth, ensure stability, reinforce the strength of expanding regional industry, and prepare to counter the threat to the economic health of the higher education industry itself. In other words, regional manpower planning fully requires the adaptability of higher education curricula and resources to contribute appropriately to regional economic development. At the same time, plans must be developed regionally and resources reallocated to maximize the strength of the higher education resource in New England. To advance the basic concept of forging a new partnership in behalf of regional economic development, the following opportunities for collaboration remain to be fully explored.

The region and states should individually and cooperatively encourage the full participation and integration of colleges, universities, and professional schools in local, state, and regional economic planning.

The region should develop an inventory of the capabilities, achievements, and resources of higher-education institutions as they relate to specific local, state, and regional issues of economic development. These characteristics, then, should be widely publicized.

Information on existing manpower shortages and the future needs of business and industry should be collected and coordinated in such a way that higher education could respond through effective planning and a continual process of updating educational programs.

In their personnel policies, including decisions on compensation and promotion, higher education institutions should take into consideration faculty research contributions to the field of state and regional economic development.

Funding sources should be sought to support directly higher participation by education in state and regional projects for economic development. A schedule of fees for service could be established where normal funding is not available to provide adequate support. Instruction in and analysis of the New England economy should be introduced into current curricula.

Universities and colleges should devote resources to identifying current and future problems in economic development and propose alternative solutions on a timely basis.

State governments should formally recognize the significant role and potential contributions of the public higher-education community to economic development by written statements in support of the idea, for example, in intent sections of proposed legislation, in study resolutions and resulting reports, and in testimony before legislative committees.

Industry and higher education should collaborate more systematically in sharing technology so that both sectors understand changes in basic and applied research and their technological impact, and the requirements of application in both educational and business terms.

Industry should play an organized and active role in providing equipment to universities and colleges aimed at visibly updating curricular capacity in response to rapidly changing technology.

Industry should support training and development programs in technological and knowledge-intensive fields, providing flexibility of instruction available at campuses, at government locations, and at company sites.

As noted in the Introduction, above, the attitude of leaders of business, government, and higher education are receptive to these ideas. What is needed now are concrete, practical steps to pursue mutual interests.

MANPOWER PLANNING

Writing in 1967, Robert W. Eisenmenger argued that "the future of New England's economy rests with the new technologically-oriented manufacturing and service industries, rather than with old-line industries such as textiles, shoes and leather, and apparel." He went on to say, as far as public policy is concerned, "New England states should place increasing emphasis on providing high-quality secondary school and college training so as to provide the necessary highly skilled labor force for the region's growing industries."[5]

A few facts about New England's labor force illustrate its national competitiveness in retaining and attracting business and industry:

The region's labor-force participation rate, particularly that of women, is higher than that of the United States as a whole, 64.8 percent to 63.2 percent. Women make up 52.2 percent of New England's work force, compared to 49.5 percent nationally.

Although at the national level only 13.9 percent of the population has completed four or more years of college, the New England rate is 16.6 percent. For completion of high school, New England's proportion is 70.4 percent to 66.6 percent for the nation overall.

Labor costs for manufacturing are 10 percent lower for New England than the national average. The level of unionization is slightly lower for New England than for the nation.[6]

New England's capital resources and highly skilled, trained labor force have made possible the growth and development of high-technology industries that serve as major exporters to national and international markets. High among the region's exports are gas turbine jet engines, electronics and computer hardware, specialized manufacturing equipment and machinery, industrial instrumentation, scientific laboratory equipment, and advanced medical instrumentation. These precision products are labor intensive and made possible by a knowledgeable, well-trained labor force.

Despite New England's dismal employment record in five of six national recessions following World War II, shifts in the region's economy since 1975 have enabled the region to outperform the nation overall in expanding the manufacturing labor force and containing the level of unemployment in the recession of 1980. From the bottom of the

1974–75 recession through March 1980, total payroll employment in New England increased at essentially the same rate as the national increase; manufacturing employment during the same period increased about 18.5 percent, compared to a national increase of 14.5 percent. This is the region's strongest employment performance since World War II.[7]

High-technology industries encompass manufacturers of computers, minicomputers, communications equipment, electronic components, guided missiles, photographic equipment, and scientific, measuring, optical, and medical instruments. Twenty-five of the top emerging high-technology growth companies are located in New England. New England now employs 16 percent of computing employees nationally, and is headquarters for 70 percent of the world's microcomputing companies, like Digital Equipment, Data General, and Wang Laboratories.

New England's employment growth of the last five years contrasts with a sluggish level of growth from 1970 to 1975, less than a third of national employment growth. Since population increased by only one percent from 1975 to 1980, the ranks of the unemployed dwindled as the regional economy expanded and shifted its emphasis to high technology and service. By the end of 1980 the national rate of unemployment had risen to 7.4 percent, while New England's stood at only 5.5 percent.

Whether New England will successfully retain its human capital and corporate resources remains to be seen. Competition from the sunbelt is fierce. Vigorous growth in high technology industries is now hindered by demand outstripping the supply of professional and technical specialists required for computer and electronic design and production. New England must not only attract from other states qualified newcomers who recognize the healthy state of the regional economy, but its institutions of higher education must provide the electronics engineers and computer scientists who are perpetually in such short supply. In Massachusetts alone, which accounts for half of the region's population and nearly half of New England's gross product, the annual shortfall is an estimated 3,000 engineers and computer scientists.

Organized labor in New England as yet has not directly concerned itself with defining the educational requirements of workers, and workplace-oriented programs have been limited. Higher education has provided limited initiative in the analysis of worker-oriented training requirements. AFL-CIO leadership in Rhode Island and Connecticut has spoken to the issue and urged increased attention to workplace education in the 1980s. However, as revealed in the New England Board of Higher Education Survey discussed in Appendix I, an area requiring significant improvement in communication and definition is the establishment of a network for labor and higher education.

When companies are relocating, even more influential than taxes, incentives, proximity to markets, and wage levels is the skilled labor force they require. Although some colleges and universities are adjusting their curricula to respond to this vital economic need of the region, a national consensus is growing in support of increased attention to training in mathematics, science, and engineering. The problem is that although high-technology companies are growing at a rate of 15 to 30 percent annually, the gradual increase of the supply of professionals and technicians does not keep pace with the surging demand.

The importance of a qualified, skilled labor force for the region is borne out by projections for the next five years by the United States Bureau of Labor Statistics.[8] The rapid-growth industries represent 38 percent of all employment in New England and include both the manufacturing and service-producing sectors. The leading manufacturing industries include electric and electronic equipment, nonelectrical machinery, and instruments. Service fields include the professional, such as medical and private educational, and such business services as management consulting. More than ever, a well-educated and trained labor force will be required to sustain projected growth of the New England economy.

Linked strongly to the growth of high-technology companies is the service-producing sector of New England's economy. While manufacturing employment declined from 38.3 percent in 1950 to 25.3 percent in 1978, the service industry grew the fastest of any sector, from 51.4 percent in 1950 to 63.9 percent in 1978. New England's service industry produces 67.5 percent of the region's real gross product, compared to 31.9 percent for manufacturing, and compared with the U.S. service industry rate of 66.7 percent. The significance of the service industry to New England's restructured economy is borne out by an M.I.T. study which found that the majority of new jobs in America are generated in newer and smaller service and trade firms, and relatively few in manufacturing. In the management consulting field alone, 23 of the top firms in the country have their headquarters in New England; another 16 maintain branch offices in the region.

STATE FUNDING OF HIGHER EDUCATION

New England provided the first university in America in 1636, in Massachusetts. New England provided the nation's first system of free public education in 1642, in Connecticut. New England was the home of Justin S. Morrill, who authored the Land-Grant College Act enacted in 1862. The six states of New England provided the earliest and most distinguished concentration of private institutions of higher learning in America. But as a result of the comparative affluence of these early institutions, the region was late in understanding the importance of investing state resources in public campuses of higher learning and in providing public support of independent private campuses of higher learning. This unfortunate circumstance, combined with escalating inflation and the slowdown in enrollments, has caused the six states to lag dramatically behind the nation in public funding of higher education.

Both the standard of living and the cost of living remain high in New England. Per capita income for New Englanders remains ahead of the national per capita income of $8,773. Though tax levels are generally high in the region, the states are still laggard in support of state-assisted colleges and universities.

In a comprehensive study of financial support of higher education for 1976 and 1977–78, published by the National Institute of Education (Tables 2 and 3), the national average for state allocation of tax revenue to public higher education was 10.6 percent. The basic patterns of that study have changed little since 1976. All New England states ranked in the bottom 10 percent of American states and the District of Columbia. While the national norm was $61.00 per capita in tax support for higher education, all New England states fell substantially below that standard.

If we compare the rankings of all American states for taxing capacity and taxing effort, however, we find only the New England states of Connecticut and New Hampshire lagging behind the national norm. Since four of the states in the region make an overall tax effort well beyond their capacity, it suggests that public higher education is not getting its fair share of state resources. The historic reliance on private higher education may have diverted the necessary attention and support required for the public sector of higher learning in the region. In the two largest states in particular, Massachusetts is allocating state funds well below the national norm for public higher education, while Connecticut

TABLE 2 State Allocation of Tax Revenue to Public Higher Education

New England States	%	National Ranking
Connecticut	6	48
Maine	7	44
Massachusetts	4	51
New Hampshire	6	47
Rhode Island	8	41
Vermont	5	50
National Average: 10.6%		

Source: Marilyn McCoy and D. Kent Halstead, *Higher Education Financing in the Fifty States,* National Institute of Education, September 1979.

TABLE 3 State and Local Appropriations to Public Institutions (per capita)

New England States	Per Capita Tax Support (dollars)	National Ranking
Connecticut	40	45
Maine	40	46
Massachusetts	36	50
New Hampshire	31	51
Rhode Island	52	31
Vermont	36	49
National average: $61.00		

is both taxing below its capacity and allocating below a fair share of the state budget its support of public higher education. It should be noted, however, that Connecticut is one of 26 states providing general appropriations to the independent sector of higher education. Also, Connecticut provides above-average financial aid to students in the independent sector.

Massachusetts provides no general appropriations to independent institutions of higher education and the lowest per-student amount of financial support of the 26 states. Maine, limited by a low tax capacity, appropriates significantly less revenue and has lower relative enrollments in the public sector than national averages. But Maine's public institutions do benefit from revenues from nonstate sources, such as federal grants and contracts, tuition, and private gifts, in amounts in excess of the national average.

Rhode Island, with a lower than average tax capacity and relatively high tax effort, also benefits from revenues from such nonstate sources as government contracts and tuition, which enable it to raise total financial support per student at public institutions to a level above the national norm. Rhode Island also ranks first in the nation in state and local appropriations to independent institutions per capita.

Similarly, New Hampshire has lower than average tax revenues and a low rate of allocation of such revenues to public higher education. But New Hampshire's public institutions, like Rhode Island's, receive above-average revenues from tuition income and government contracts, bringing total educational and general revenues per student above the national norm.

Vermont, which has a relatively low tax capacity and high tax effort, allocates a low proportion of its tax revenues to public higher education and augments its low level of assistance to public institutions with high levels of tuition revenue and government contract revenue. The result brings total educational and general revenues per student in the public sector significantly above the national norm (Table 4).

TABLE 4. Tax Performance of New England States

	State Tax Capacity			State Tax Effort	
	$ Per Capita	Index	Rank	Index	Rank
Connecticut	727	113	7	95	20
Maine	476	70	51	118	7
Massachusetts	605	94	31	131	2
New Hampshire	627	97	29	80	43
Rhode Island	553	86	42	115	9
Vermont	542	84	44	121	3
United States	643	100.0		100.0	

Finally, it must be pointed out that the entry rate of New England residents into their respective state institutions of higher education falls well below the national norm of 59 percent. New Hampshire's 30 percent rate is the lowest in the nation, while Oregon has the nation's highest rate of 132 percent.

Since the college entry rate indicates the degree to which a state's high school graduates find public higher education in their state attractive and are financially able to attend, important questions are raised for New England's state policy makers (Table 5). Whereas in the past, students have been able to go to out-of-state colleges at a reasonable cost, increasing numbers are now attending schools in their home states. Each of the six states should evaluate the programs and curricula in their public institutions of higher learning to determine whether they appeal to the new pools of students interested in attending lower-cost public colleges. Student, parental, and community attitudes toward attendance in the public sector are worthy of careful examination. Further, it is imperative to analyze whether students are adequately prepared and counseled for higher education opportunities and, on the other hand, whether admissions and financial aid policies and procedures widen student access (Table 5).

TABLE 5. Entry Rate to Public Institutions

State	Entry Rate* (percentages)	National Ranking
Connecticut	43	36
Maine	36	45
Massachusetts	44	31
New Hampshire	30	51
Rhode Island	33	50
Vermont	38	43
United States	59	

*First-time resident enrollment in public institutions as a percentage of high school graduates.

TABLE 6. In-Migration to Public Institutions (per 1,000 population)

New England States	In-Migration	National Ranking
Vermont	2.4	5
New Hampshire	1.8	8
Rhode Island	.9	31
Maine	.9	32
Massachusetts	.5	45
Connecticut	.5	46

A national comparison of in-migration of nonresidents enrolling in public institutions also reveals that New England's two largest states, Massachusetts and Connecticut, lag well behind the national standard in providing attractive, accessible public higher education to out-of-state students (Table 6). These two states should evaluate why their public institutions fall significantly below the national norm, in view of such factors as the level of nonresident tuition, academic reputation, offerings, climate, and the degree of competition for nonresident students from nearby states. The national average is almost one person (.9) per 1,000 traveling to another state for higher education, with sunbelt states leading the country in enrolling out-of-state students and frostbelt states having the fewest number of out-of-staters (Table 7).

New England's emphasis on independent higher education is borne out by budget and enrollment figures. Two thirds of all expenditures for public and private higher education are by independent institutions. In considering the number of fulltime, enrolled students per 1,000 population at all institutions of higher learning in each of the six states, we find that every New England state except Maine ranks substantially above

TABLE 7. FTE Enrollment in Independent and Public Institutions (per 1,000 population)

New England States	Independent Enrollment	Public Enrollment	
		Numbers	National Ranking
Connecticut	13.3	21.6	47
Maine	8.3	22.3	44
Massachusetts	28.7	21.9	45
New Hampshire	18.3	23.5	41
Rhode Island	29.7	24.6	38
Vermont	23.7	29.2	27
United States	9.0	29.8	

the national norm for the independent sector and significantly below the national norm in every state but Vermont for the public sector.

In its view of higher education, New England is oriented to its highly developed private sector. The orientation is not exactly reciprocal. The region's independent higher-education resource, however distinguished, seems disinclined on the whole to revise curricula in conformity with area manpower needs. Even the prospect of an expanding economy, in which new forms of technical and professional training are required, seems unlikely to persuade most private institutions to identify fully with regional development. The public sector, on the other hand, has a clear mandate to address public needs. Accordingly, it becomes more critical for state institutions to exercise adaptiveness and flexibility in responding to the demand for well-trained manpower in the region.

This decade is destined to experience the impact of major revisions of economic theories and applications accumulated since World War II. Higher education will continue to play a vital role in the process of redefinition. The opportunity of extending its own contribution beyond the realms of theory and research as active participant and potential partner in creating regional economic development policy is a distinct possibility in New England, where the educational resource is a determining factor in the health of the economy itself. Higher education in New England has the potential of serving as both catalyst and active participant. The engagement of the region's colleges and universities as not merely consultants and analysts but as providers and accountable partners in the process of reinvigoration is a decision worthy of most serious consideration by the higher-educational community.

Concern for economic development will dominate the decade, and higher education will continue to lose ground if it remains aloof from the issues, the complex process of problem resolution, and appropriate engagement with developmental strategies.

The perception of business, government, and labor is fairly close to a consensus that higher education must be willing to become participant observers in the economic struggle. Such action will require considerable change in the traditional stance of observational reserve and detached analysis which has been the privileged role of the higher education community.

3. MARKET INFLUENCES ON HIGHER EDUCATION: A PERSPECTIVE FOR THE 1980s

Peter B. Doeringer
Patricia Flynn Pannell
Pankaj Tandon

The New England economy has undergone a substantial transformation since World War II as durable manufacturing and commercial services have replaced mill-based industry. These changes have not always been easily accommodated. For example, loss of jobs in rural areas and older mill towns held down economic growth in New England, and sudden surges in the demand for skilled and highly educated labor from time to time have left many companies short-handed for substantial periods. Despite these problems of adjustment, the experience of the 1970s suggests that the New England economy has absorbed much of the impact of industrial decline and that its economy is now surprisingly resilient.

Alongside these changes in the economy have been shifts in higher education. The scientific and business orientation of higher education has grown substantially; two-year degree programs have blossomed; and university-based research and development has become a major industry.

The purpose of this paper is to examine these changes in the New England economy, to explore their implications for higher education, to suggest how higher education may contribute to economic development, and to identify areas of concern for higher-education policy in the 1980s.

THE CONTRIBUTION OF HIGHER EDUCATION TO ECONOMIC DEVELOPMENT

In recent years it has been fashionable for colleges and universities to account for their economic contribution to the community. Payrolls, local purchases of goods and services, and estimates of the spending

The authors would like to express their gratitude to Susan Jones, who contributed the section on models of research dissemination, and Mary Tondreau, who served as a research assistant.

power of students paint an impressive revenue picture. Such an exercise, however important, is not the focus of this chapter. The intention, rather, is to examine the role of higher education as a sector of the economy producing services for the region and beyond.

Higher education serves two distinct markets. In the labor market it provides education to be "purchased" and "consumed" by students, and it contributes to employers by building the nation's skilled labor supply. In the research and development market it conducts research needed to generate technological advances.

The contribution of education to economic development has been approached in a variety of ways. It has been estimated that historically, education has contributed almost one third to growth of per-capita income in the United States economy.[1] Such a conclusion is reinforced by the "human capital" literature, showing that education can be understood as an investment process whereby individuals acquire schooling which then pays dividends in the form of higher productivity and pay.[2]

Another area where education has made a contribution is technical progress. As with education, research and development can be seen as an investment leading to higher productivity and growth. Estimates suggest that about half of the growth in per-capita income can be traced to such progress. Taken together, over three fourths of per-capita income growth can be traced back to knowledge and its application.[3]

Research universities have always played an important part in basic and applied research. There is a long record of patents and prizes commemorating the contribution of university research to both theoretical and practical advances in science, medicine, business, and law. It is often suggested that such universities also act as a magnet attracting companies seeking ready access to research talent and resources. Less well known is the direct participation of faculty in spinning off new business ventures. Analyses of R & D investment in general have shown it to yield reasonable rates of return, but little is known specifically about university-based R & D.

Though higher education has undoubtedly had an important function in the economy historically, there have been troublesome developments during the 1970s. Criticisms have been launched from the left that higher education has inappropriately helped to secure leadership positions for the economic and political elite.[4] Corporations have complained that higher education has failed to respond adequately to employment needs in industry. Students have felt that higher education has not been sufficiently vocational.[5] Foundations have supported extensive reexamination of the performance and direction of higher education.

The markets for higher education have deteriorated substantially. The boom in enrollments of the 1960s tapered off by the late 1970s, and declines are projected for the 1980s.[6] While much attention has been paid to figuring out how higher education will adapt to this future decline, the unrealized employment expectations of many recent graduates is already dampening higher education enrollments.

Recession has also been felt in higher education's second market, research and development. Support for R & D has declined in real terms in the last decade. Not only has this decline affected higher education budgets, but it may also explain some of the recent deterioration in productivity and technical progress observed in the United States.[7]

These developments suggest that the problem of the higher-education sector in the 1980s may be larger than one of declining enrollments. A broad range of institutional goals and performance may also be at issue.

The quality of the performance of institutions of higher education is rarely studied directly or systematically. Usually the assumption is made that if such performance measures as enrollments, financial solvency, and grant and contract activity are being maintained, institutional performance need not be questioned. These market tests may be appropriate for an era when higher education was principally striving to meet the educational aspirations of students. If, however, higher education is to be judged in terms of its contribution to economic development, different criteria of performance may be needed.

In this spirit a set of questions about the place of the higher education sector in the economy are posed in this paper. Is there a positive impact of higher education beyond payrolls, purchases, and the fulfilling of students' educational aspirations? Are there unmet needs for educated labor that constrain growth? Is the expansion of support for research and technical assistance in the higher education sector likely to stimulate economic advances? If the answer to any of these questions is in the affirmative, where should resources be allocated, what types of institutional behavior should be encouraged, and how should the higher education system be reorganized to meet these challenges? If higher education is to become more responsive to the needs of the economy, will this conflict with other educational goals and values?

Although there is no shortage of opinions about the answers to these questions, there is no consensus, and surprisingly little solid evidence has been marshaled to support contending views. To address these questions the postwar trends in the New England economy and their implications for higher education are reviewed in the next section, followed by an examination of the responsiveness of the education system to labor markets and to R & D needs.

THE CHANGING STRUCTURE OF THE NEW ENGLAND ECONOMY

The New England economy has undergone substantial changes during the postwar period. Some of these changes, such as the shift away from manufacturing, parallel movements in the national economy. Others, such as the decline in shoes and textiles, reflect the unique history of the New England economy.

During the period 1947–79, nonagricultural employment in New England rose by 62 percent, about one third less than the nation as a whole (Table 1). This growth, however, was spread unevenly. Manufacturing employment, for instance, which accounted for almost half of the area's employment in 1947, declined slightly in absolute terms and comprised only about one quarter of New England jobs by 1979. Within the manufacturing sector there was a significant shift away from employment in nondurable goods, with the bulk of the job loss occurring in textiles, leather, food, and apparel. While durable manufacturing experienced less than average growth within the region, transportation equipment, electrical machinery, and instruments all grew well above average. Nonmanufacturing employment in New England more than doubled. Services showed the largest rate of growth, more than tripling, followed by government and finance, insurance, and real estate (Table 1). By 1979 the New England area was service oriented, with over two thirds of the region's employment in service-producing industries (Table 2).

Although the New England area is shifting away from manufacturing and into the service-producing areas faster than the nation as a whole, employment in the region remains more concentrated in manufacturing than for the United States as a whole. In addition, New England now has a higher percentage of its jobs in services, finance, insurance, and real estate than does the rest of the nation. In contrast, New England has a

TABLE 1. Nonagricultural Industrial Employment in New England (1947–1979)

Industry	1947 (000's)	1979 (000's)	Change in Total Number of Jobs (000's)	% Change	U.S. % Change
Nonagricultural total	3,332	5,935	+2,063	+62	+105
Manufacturing total	1,544	1,522	–22	–1	+35
Durable Manufacturing	683	924	+241	+35	+52
Lumber and wood	48	32	–16	–33	–9
Furniture and fixtures	18	20	+2	+11	+49
Stone, clay, and glass	21	32	+11	+52	+32
Primary metals	73	52	–21	–29	–3
Fabricated metal products	119	144	+25	+21	+74
Machinery (except electrical)	190	203	+13	+7	+81
Electrical machinery	112	205	+93	+83	+105
Transportation equipment	58	138	+80	+138	+63
Instruments	44	98	+54	+123	+58
Nondurable Manufacturing	861	598	–263	–31	+16
Food	86	60	–26	–30	–4
Textile mill products	280	64	–216	–77	–32
Apparel	87	65	–22	–25	+14
Paper and allied products	72	70	–2	–3	+52
Printing and publishing	55	87	+32	+58	+72
Chemicals and allied products	28	42	+14	+50	+71
Rubber products	59	71	+12	+20	+140
Leather and leather products	114	58	–56	–49	–40
Misc. manufacturing	80	81	+1	+1	

TABLE 1 *(continued)*

Industry	1947 (000's)	1979 (000's)	Change in Total Number of Jobs (000's)	% Change	U.S. % Change
Nonmanufacturing total	1,788	3,873	+2,085	+117	+143
Construction	127	190	+63	+50	+123
Transportation and public utilities	228	236	+8	+4	+23
Trade (wholesale and retail)	599	1,160	+561	+94	+126
Finance, insurance, and real estate	129	312	+183	+142	+188
Services and misc.	368	1,138	+770	+209	+240
Government	337	837	+500	+148	+191

Sources: U.S. Dept. of Labor, Bureau of Labor Statistics, "A Generation of Change in the New England Employment Structure, 1947–1979" (Boston: New England Regional Office, 1980).

U.S. Dept. of Labor, Bureau of Labor Statistics, "The Changing Structure of New England Employment, 1947–1973" (Boston: New England Regional Office, 1974).

"Employment by Industry Group and Major Manufacturing Group," *Monthly Labor Review* (October 1980), p. 74.

TABLE 2. Distribution of Nonagricultural Industrial Employment in New England and the United States

(1947, 1979)

Industry	1947 N.E.	1947 U.S.	1979 N.E.	1979 U.S.
Nonagricultural total	100.0%	100.0%	100.0%	100.0%
Manufacturing total	46.3	35.4	28.2	23.4
Durable total	20.5	19.1	17.7	14.2
Nondurable total	28.5	16.3	11.1	9.3
Nonmanufacturing total	53.7	64.6	71.8	76.6
Mining		2.2		1.1
Construction	3.8	4.6	3.5	5.2
Transportation and public utilities	6.8	9.5	4.4	5.8
Trade	18.0	20.4	21.5	22.5
Fire	3.9	3.9	5.8	5.5
Service	11.1	11.5	21.1	19.0
Government	10.1	12.5	15.5	17.5

Sources: U.S. Department of Labor, Bureau of Labor Statistics, "A Generation of Change in the New England Employment Structure, 1947–79" (Boston: New England Regional Office, 1980).

U.S. Department of Labor, Bureau of Labor Statistics, "The Changing Structure of New England Employment, 1947–73" (Boston: New England Regional Office, 1974).

Employment and Training Report of the President, 1980, p. 305.

disproportionately small share of its jobs in government, construction, transportation, and public utilities. In many respects New England's mix of manufacturing and nonmanufacturing work is becoming more like the nation's, but its growth pattern suggests that during the 1980s it will be leading the nation in its service orientation.

Despite a poor record of growth, the vast changes in the industrial structure within the region over this period may have resulted in a more diversified and viable economy. In terms of employment as a percentage of population and real per-capita income, New England outperformed the United States. Since 1977 the region's unemployment rates have remained below those of the country as a whole.[8]

Trends in industrial employment show the general direction in which the economy is moving. In New England, for example, services and trade are expected to continue growing relatively fast, while nondurable manufacturing is expected to continue its decline (Table 3). Because

TABLE 3. Projected Changes in Nonagricultural Employment by Industry for New England

(1974–1985)

Industry	1974	1985	Absolute Change 1974–85	% Change 1974–85
Nonagricultural total	4,975,669	5,475,054	+499,385	+9.6
Manufacturing total	1,431,677	1,420,955	-10,722	-0.8
Durable goods total	905,076	927,639	+22,563	+2.5
Ordinance	29,361	30,130	+769	+2.6
Lumber and wood	32,584	28,942	-3,642	-11.2
Furniture and fixtures	22,765	22,782	+17	+0.1
Stone, clay, and glass	30,714	33,045	+2,331	+7.6
Primary metals	53,576	48,396	-5,180	-9.7
Fabricated metal products	125,112	133,421	+8,309	+6.6
Machinery (except electrical)	173,011	178,509	+5,498	+3.2
Electrical machinery	182,430	188,322	+5,892	+3.2
Transportation	112,596	116,444	+3,848	+3.4
Instruments	69,554	75,533	+5,979	+8.6
Misc. manufacturing	73,373	72,115	-1,258	-1.7
Nondurable goods total	526,601	493,316	-33,285	-6.3
Food	62,179	53,276	-8,903	-14.3
Tobacco	428	431	+3	+0.7
Textile mill products	70,603	57,577	-13,026	-18.5
Apparel	67,143	52,084	-15,059	-22.4
Paper and allied products	70,781	68,750	-2,031	-2.9
Printing and publishing	82,632	90,278	+7,646	+9.3
Chemicals and allied products	39,645	42,748	+3,103	+7.8
Petroleum	1,990	1,996	+6	+0.3
Rubber products	73,737	79,015	+5,278	+7.2
Leather and leather products	57,463	47,161	-10,302	-17.9
Nonmanufacturing total				
Mining	3,592	3,764	+172	+4.8
Construction	295,215	333,293	+38,078	+12.9
Transportation and public utilities	256,896	270,012	+13,116	+5.1
Trade (wholesale and retail)	1,088,148	1,240,084	+151,936	+14.0
Finance, insurance, and real estate	287,203	339,145	+51,942	+18.1
Services	1,376,578	1,604,031	+227,453	+16.5
Government	236,360	263,770	+27,410	+11.6

Source: U.S. Department of Labor, Bureau of Labor Statistics, *Projections of Industrial Employment in New England to 1985* (Boston: New England Regional Office, 1977).

individuals are trained to enter occupations, not industries, occupational data is much more central to defining training needs.

OCCUPATIONAL TRENDS

Data on employment by occupation in New England 1960–70 shows professional and technical jobs leading the expansion of the economy (Table 4). Service, clerical, managerial, and administrative occupations also experienced faster than average growth, while there was a decline in the number of operative and farm jobs in the region.

This large increase in professional and technical jobs was similar to the national trend. Several other regional changes, however, were significantly different from those occurring nationally. For instance, the New England economy far out-paced the nation in its growth of managers, administrators, and service workers. In addition, operative jobs in New England declined, while nationally they rose slightly. Craft jobs in New England increased but to a much smaller extent than nationally.

By 1970 over half of the region's workers were in white collar occupations. New England still had a larger share of its workers in operative and craft occupations than the nation as a whole, but by 1970 it also had a disproportionately larger percentage of its employment in professional and technical, managerial, administrative, and clerical jobs (Table 5).

Occupational projections indicate a continuation of past trends. White collar jobs in New England are expected to continue a faster than average growth through 1985, accounting for over 70 percent of the new jobs (Table 6). Clerical occupations will be the most rapidly growing within this group. Craft, operative, and farm jobs will continue to decline, while growth will continue among service workers. By 1985 it is estimated that the region's occupational structure will bear a striking similarity to that of the nation.

It is important to keep in mind that these projections incorporate trends only through 1974 and do not capture such unanticipated developments as the rapid growth in high-technology employment. Of even greater significance is the fact that these projections indicate only *new* jobs, that is net *growth* in demand. They do not represent the expected number of job *openings*, which also include replacement needs due to turnover, death, and retirement.

In fact one finds that the majority of all anticipated job openings in the early 1980s in each of the six New England states are expected to be the

TABLE 4. Occupation of Employed Persons in New England (1960, 1970)

Occupation	New England 1960	New England 1970	Employment 1960–70	Percent 1960–70[a]	United States Percent 1960–70
Total, all occupations	4,034,647	4,750,972	716,325	+17.8	+18.4
Professional, technical, kindred	487,792	786,381	298,589	+61.2	+56.9
Managers, administrators, except farm	317,020	405,060	88,040	+27.8	+17.8
Sales workers	282,161	321,383	39,222	+13.9	+17.3
Clerical and kindred	615,519	881,826	266,307	+43.3	+47.7
Craftsmen, foremen and kindred workers	588,641	666,735	78,094	+13.3	+21.4
Operatives	906,168	895,299	-10,869	-1.2	+13.1
Laborers, except farm	153,595	178,547	24,952	+16.2	+10.3
Farmers and farm workers	68,834	44,112	-24,722	-35.9	-39.8
Service workers (including private household)	390,308	571,629	181,321	+46.4	+36.3
Occupation not reported	224,609				

[a]Because of the nonclassification of 224,609 (5.6%) occupations in 1960, some of these percentage changes will be overstated.

Sources: U.S. Department of Commerce, Census of the Population, 1960, U.S. Summary, Table 126, "Occupation Group of Employed Males, by Regions, Divisions and States: 1960"; and Table 127, "Occupation Group of Employed Females, by Regions, Divisions and States: 1960."

U.S. Department of Commerce, Census of the Population, 1970, Table 165, "Occupation of Employed Persons for Regions, Divisions, and States: 1970."

TABLE 5. Percentage Distribution of Employment by Occupation in New England and in the United States (1960, 1970, 1985)

Occupation	New England 1960[a]	New England 1970	New England Projected 1985[b]	United States 1960	United States 1970	United States Projected 1985[b]
Professional and technical	12.8	16.6	15.4	11.8	14.8	15.9
Managers and administrators	8.3	8.5	10.5	8.8	8.3	11.1
Sales	7.4	6.8	6.1	7.5	7.1	6.3
Clerical	16.2	18.6	19.5	15.1	17.9	19.0
Craftsmen	15.5	14.0	13.3	14.2	13.9	13.6
Operatives	23.8	18.8	14.7	19.4	17.6	15.6
Laborers	4.0	3.8	4.6	5.1	4.5	4.2
Farmers	1.8	0.9	1.8	6.4	3.1	0.5
Service workers	10.2	12.0	14.1	11.7	12.8	13.8
Total	100.0	100.0	100.0	100.0	100.0	100.0

[a]Distribution of those reported; 224,609 (5.6%) occupations in 1960 were not classified.

[b]Calculated using 1974 employment base.

Sources: U.S. Department of Commerce, Census of the Population, 1960, U.S. Summary, Table 126, "Occupation Group of Employed Males, by Regions, Divisions, and States: 1960," and Table 127, "Occupation Group of Employed Females, by Regions, Divisions, and States: 1960."

U.S. Department of Commerce, Census of the Population, 1970, Table 165, "Occupation of Employed Persons for Regions, Divisions, and States: 1970."

Leonard Lecht, *Changes in Occupational Characteristics: Planning Ahead for the 1980's* (New York: The Conference Board, 1976), Appendix B, Table B-3.

result of replacements (Table 7). New Hampshire has the lowest proportion of total openings as the result of separations, while in Connecticut almost three quarters of the projected openings are due to replacement.

RESPONSIVENESS OF HIGHER EDUCATION TO EMPLOYMENT TRENDS

Surprisingly little is known about how higher education in New England has responded to these economic trends through changes in enrollment by field and discipline. Detailed data by region has only recently become available, and regional enrollment projections are nonexistent.

These data limitations are understandable, given that most graduates

TABLE 6. Projected Changes in Major Occupational Classifications in New England and the United States

(1974–1985)

Occupation	1974 (000's)	1985 (000's)	Average Annual Absolute Change 1974–85 (000's)	Average Annual % Change 1974–85	U.S. Average Annual % Change 1974–85
Total, all occupations	5,054	5,537	+483	+0.9	+1.8
White collar workers	2,562	2,901	+339	+1.2	+2.5
Professional and technical workers	795	881	+86	+0.9	+2.7
Managers, officials and proprietors	552	613	+61	+1.0	+2.0
Sales workers	310	349	+39	+1.1	+1.4
Clerical workers	906	1,059	+153	+1.5	+3.1
Blue collar workers	2,492	2,636	+144	+0.5	+1.2
Craft and kindred workers	689	755	+66	+0.9	+1.8
Operatives	876	863	-13	-0.1	+0.8
Service workers	659	761	+102	+1.4	+2.5
Nonfarm laborers	223	231	+8	+0.3	+0.8
Farmers and farm workers	46	27	-19	-3.8	-3.5

Sources: U.S. Department of Labor, Bureau of Labor Statistics, *Projections of Occupational Employment in New England to 1985* (Boston: New England Regional Office, 1978).

L. Lecht, *Changes in Occupational Characteristics: Planning Ahead for the 1980's* (New York: The Conference Board, 1976), Appendix B, Table B-3.

of the higher-education sector face national rather than regional labor markets. Moreover, career choices, and therefore educational projections, depend crucially on such unstable factors as employment prospects and financial assistance for students. The important comparisons, as a result, involve supply and demand not only in New England but in the country at large. From this perspective the educated labor pool available to New England can be adjusted either through enrollment changes or by changing the share of the national supply captured by employers in the region.

Manpower gaps in the regional economy can therefore be understood in two ways. The first is to take projections of national and regional

TABLE 7. Percentage of Annual Job Openings Due to Replacement Demand in the Six New England States

(1980–1982)[a]

Occupation	CT	ME	MA	NH	RI	VT
Professional and technical	70.3	60.1	64.3	46.1	73.5	60.4
Managers and administrators	70.6	60.9	67.1	49.9	69.1	66.2
Sales	71.4	55.9	72.4	53.5	72.8	68.0
Clerical workers	66.5	59.7	61.5	52.3	63.9	56.4
Crafts and kindred	81.3	58.1	64.9	n.a.[b]	68.6	56.0
Operatives	88.3	52.0	72.5	n.a.[b]	68.2	58.5
Service workers	70.0	53.4	67.8	59.5	70.4	69.3
Laborers (except farm)	82.5	51.9	70.8	n.a.[b]	75.0	73.4
Farmers and farm workers	100.0	n.a.[b]	100.0	n.a.[b]	100.0	100.0
All occupations	73.4	56.4	67.0	54.2	69.1	65.2

[a]This Table is based on the individual state's employment projections, which are produced for different time periods and with different base years—but all of which include projected annual demands for 1980–82.

[b]New Hampshire occupational categories differ from those of the other states. In addition to occupations listed on the table, data are available for the following:

Agriculture, fishery and forestry	67.2%
Processing occupations	65.8
Machine trade occupations	61.7
Bench work occupations	67.0
Structural work occupations	54.9
Miscellaneous occupations	49.9
Other blue collar occupations	57.7

Sources: Connecticut Labor Department, Employment Security Division, Office of Research and Information, *Annual Planning Information, Fiscal Year 1981, Connecticut,* July 1980.

Maine Department of Manpower Affairs, Bureau of Employment Security, Manpower Research Division, *Maine Occupational Outlook to 1982,* April 1980.

Massachusetts Division of Employment Security, Job Market Research, *Employment Requirements by Occupation, by Industry, 1976–1985,* December 1979.

New Hampshire Department of Employment Security, *New Hampshire Employment by Occupation Projected to 1990,* November 1979.

Rhode Island Department of Employment Security, *Rhode Island Occupational Projections to 1985.*

Vermont Department of Employment Security, Research and Statistics Section, *Vermont Employment Projections to 1985,* April 1979.

employment changes and compare them to enrollments by field to identify shortage areas. Various assumptions can then be made about possible changes in the region's expected share of the labor supply. Because this approach assumes relatively stable staffing and pay arrangements, it is the more conservative way of looking at future labor market conditions. It ignores a number of adjustments and substitutions that normally occur in such markets in the face of perceived shortages. Unfilled vacancies place pressure upon salaries and interfere with production. Employers in turn react by "economizing" on scarce skills, reorganizing tasks, and tapping substitute labor pools.

The second approach is more dynamic. It recognizes that economizing on labor will blunt projected labor demand. Substitutions of one type of labor for another will make short-term skill supplies more elastic than enrollment data would indicate. Rising salaries will raise the rate of return on skill acquisition and will feed back into career and education decisions, thereby causing longer-term increases in the labor supply.

These dynamic accommodations to labor scarcity will gradually close the manpower gap without further assistance from public policy. For employers, however, these adjustments may carry drawbacks—paying higher salaries, changing staffing patterns, and hiring "second-choice" employees. Moreover, these market-induced adjustments take time. While minor shortages can be accommodated, more substantial shortages, particularly in scientific fields, can be resolved only through shifts in school enrollments. These long-term supply adjustments can take years or even decades. Meanwhile, salaries and labor costs may be abnormally high and production may be hampered.

Equally disturbing is the problem of labor surpluses, which can emerge after protracted periods of scarcity. Career and education choices are strongly influenced by the recent record of pay and job opportunities. Rarely, however, do students adjust their career expectations on the basis of the effects of students already in the educational pipeline. The greater the shortage, the better employment prospects appear and the more likely a future labor surplus as students flock to lucrative careers.

Numerous studies have documented the tendency toward imbalances in the labor market for the highly educated.[9] Engineering and science fields in particular show regular cycles of supply and demand imbalances because of sudden shifts in demand, long training times, and the lack of staffing alternatives.

Interestingly, these cycles are often aggravated by public policy. In the case of the aerospace boom of the 1950s and 1960s, for example, the stimulus to enrollments of rising salaries and job vacancies in aerospace sciences was reinforced by lucrative training fellowships provided by the government. Enrollments grew dramatically between 1953 and 1968, but the demand for new graduates tapered off once the rapid aerospace buildup was completed in the mid 1960s and the job market became seriously depressed.[10]

CHANGES IN EDUCATIONAL OUTPUT

Understanding how well the higher-education system in New England responds to changing labor needs requires the examination of trends in graduates by level and field. Nationally, higher education expanded rapidly in the 1960s and early 1970s. Growth patterns differed markedly, however, between the decades of the 1960s and the 1970s.

During the 1960s, for example, bachelor degrees awarded rose 2½ times, peaking in 1973–74 (Table 8). Social science degrees more than tripled; biological sciences, accounting, agriculture, and natural resource degrees more than doubled; while degrees in the natural sciences and engineering grew much more slowly.

Growth of degrees at this level slowed to 10 percent in the first half of the 1970s, and a very different pattern emerged. Social science degrees rose a mere 4 percent, while humanities degrees declined slightly. Unlike the 1960s, the natural sciences and miscellaneous fields did relatively well, expanding by 16 percent. Degrees in health and computer and information systems more than doubled during this period. In addition, accounting, agriculture, and biological science degrees each grew relatively fast. In contrast, degrees in mathematics, education, and engineering fell by 36 percent, 12 percent, and 7 percent respectively.

Masters and doctoral degrees rose rapidly throughout the 1960s but, unlike bachelor degrees, grew more slowly rather than declining in the 1970s.[11] Computers, health, business, and management were the major growth areas, education degrees continued to rise, and engineering peaked in the early 1970s and then began to slide.

The number of associate degrees conferred in the early to mid–1970s rose by about two thirds.[12] Health services and paramedical degrees almost tripled. Business and commerce, natural science technology, and the science and engineering occupational fields more than doubled. Mechanical and engineering technology degrees rose by two thirds, while data processing, the arts and sciences, and general programs showed the slowest growth.

Regional and national data on enrollment by fields classify only about one third of all students in higher education.[13] Even these limited data reveal differences between New England and the United States. For example, a much higher percentage of New England students are in

TABLE 8. Earned Bachelors' Degrees, with Projections, by Field of Study, United States (1960-61–1986-87)

Curriculum	Average Annual Percentage of Change 1960–61 to 1970–71	Average Annual Percentage of Change 1970–71 to 1975–76	Average Annual Percentage of Change 1975–76 to 1986–87	Number of Degrees Earned 1975–1976	Peak Year 1960–61 to 1975–76	Projected Peak Year 1976–77 to 1986–87
Total social sciences	+24.2	+0.8	+0.4	213,853	1973–74	1982–83
Total humanities	+17.8	–0.0	–0.3	139,552	1973–74	1976–77
Total natural sciences and miscellaneous fields	+9.0	+3.2	+0.7	572,341	1975–76	1982–83
Mathematics	+8.9	–7.2	–0.6	15,984	1969–70	1976–77
Computer and information systems	—	+27.4	+10.1	5,652	1975–76	1986–87
Engineering	+3.3	–1.4	+4.4	46,331	1972–73	1982–83
Physical sciences	+3.9	+0.0	+0.1	21,465	1968–69	1982–83
Biological sciences	+12.5	+10.2	+2.5	54,275	1975–76	1984–85
Agriculture and natural resources	+10.2	+10.6	+0.9	19,402	1975–76	1983–84
Health professions	+9.6	+22.8	+3.8	53,958	1975–76	1985–86
Accounting	+10.9	+12.4	+1.2	35,806	1975–76	1982–83
Business and management	+13.1	+3.0	+0.7	107,630	1975–76	1983–84
Education	+9.4	–2.4	–2.3	154,758	1972–73	1976–77
Other	+8.2	+18.6	+1.1	57,080	1975–76	1984–85
Total, all curricula	+12.7	+2.0	+0.5	925,746	1973–74	1982–83

Source: National Center for Education Statistics, *Projections of Education Statistics to 1986–87* (Washington, D.C.: U.S. Government Printing Office, 1978), pp. 42–44.

business and management than nationally. New England also accounts for a disproportionately large percentage of agriculture and natural resources, engineering, and law students. In contrast New England provides training to relatively few architectural, dental, and medical students (Table 9).

Slight growth is predicted into the mid–1980s in the number of bachelor degrees conferred.[14] The natural sciences and health fields are expected to continue to do relatively well. Computer and information-systems degrees are projected to continue their expansion, doubling again by 1986–87. In contrast, humanities, education, and mathematics degrees are expected to decline throughout the period. Engineering degrees are expected to rebound.

At the post-baccalaureate levels, the education, business and management, and health fields, are projected to continue a relatively fast expansion, but engineering degrees are expected to fall (Table 10). These projections depend, however, on assumptions about salaries and employment which may become increasingly obsolete with changes in the economy.

IMBALANCES IN THE LABOR MARKET

Having examined the changing structure of employment and the shifts in the size and composition of college graduates nationally, some selected comparisons will be made to highlight areas of potential shortages and surpluses.

Engineering. Historically, the supply of college-trained engineers has fluctuated widely as students adjusted to changing labor market conditions. As noted in Table 8, engineering degrees rose 33 percent in the 1960s but fell in the 1970s, under the influence of the deteriorating employment conditions that prevailed in the late 1960s and early 1970s. As enrollment declined, however, the demand for engineers revived in the late 1970s. The net result is a current shortage of engineers.

Students are once again responding to improved job and salary conditions. The supply of engineering degrees is projected to rise by almost 50 percent between 1975 and 1985.[15] Shortages are expected to shrink but will still be felt well into the mid–1980s as employment needs continue to expand.

Computer specialists. The market for computer specialists has been very strong throughout the 1960s and 1970s. Employment is expected to continue growing well above average.

TABLE 9. Total Enrollments in Institutions of Higher Education by Field, New England Versus United States (1978)

Degree Field	New England		United States		New England Enrollment as % of United States
	Enrollment	%	Enrollment	%	
Agriculture and natural resources	9,395	1.3	104,212	0.9	9.0
Architecture and environmental design	3,103	0.4	66,371	0.6	4.7
Biological science	17,106	2.4	301,868	2.7	5.7
Business and management	122,051	17.2	1,509,127	13.3	8.1
Engineering	40,353	5.7	521,578	4.6	7.7
Dentistry	720	0.1	22,034	0.2	3.3
Medicine	2,999	0.4	67,055	0.6	4.5
Veterinary medicine	0	0.0	7,186	0.1	0.0
Law	9,490	1.4	119,120	1.0	8.0
Physical sciences	10,323	1.5	164,314	1.4	6.3
All other	493,030	69.6	8,465,305	74.6	5.8
Total	708,570	100.0	11,348,170	100.0	6.2

Source: A. J. Pepin, National Center for Education Statistics, *Fall Enrollment in Higher Education, 1978* (Washington, D.C.: U.S. Government Printing Office, 1979), pp. 190–191.

TABLE 10. Pecentage Distribution of Earned Degrees by Field of Study and Level: United States (1964-65–1986-87)

Curriculum	Bachelor			Master			Doctor		
	1964–65	1975–76	1986–87	1964–65	1975–76	1986–87	1964–65	1975–76	1986–87
Social sciences	19.8	23.1	22.8	16.0	16.0	13.8	16.9	21.5	22.9
Humanities	16.0	15.1	13.8	12.1	9.6	9.2	11.2	12.4	11.8
Natural sciences and miscellaneous fields	64.2	61.8	63.4	71.9	74.4	77.0	71.9	66.1	65.3
Mathematics	3.9	1.7	1.5	3.6	1.2	1.0	4.1	2.5	2.0
Computer and information systems	a	0.6	1.2	0.1	0.8	1.5	a	0.7	1.1
Engineering	7.7	5.0	7.0	10.3	5.2	3.7	13.0	8.3	5.9
Health professions	3.1	5.8	7.8	2.1	4.0	5.1	1.0	1.7	2.1
Accounting	3.0	3.9	4.1	0.5	0.9	0.9	0.2	0.2	0.1
Business and management	9.6	11.6	11.8	6.0	12.8	14.6	1.8	2.6	3.1
Education	23.2	16.7	11.9	37.0	41.0	42.8	16.3	22.8	27.6

[a] Less than 0.05 percent.

Source: National Center for Education Statistics, *Projections of Education Statistics to 1986–87* (Washington, D.C.: U.S. Government Printing Office, 1978), pp. 40–41.

Unlike the supply of new engineering degree recipients, computer and information systems degrees have been steadily climbing in the past two decades. Supply is growing at a faster rate than demand; however, it still falls short of labor market needs. As would be expected, labor market shortfalls are being met more rapidly in computer jobs requiring relatively less skill. For example, the market for keypunchers and console operators is already becoming saturated, while the market for computer programmers is not expected to come into balance until the mid–1980s. The demand for systems analysts far surpasses the supply of new college graduates and, if current trends continue, shortages will continue beyond the mid–1980s.

Business and management occupations. Employment in managerial and administrative positions rose 18 percent from 1960 to 1970.[16] Between 1974 and 1985, growth is projected to be slightly higher than average.[17] The supply of business and management graduates expanded throughout the 1960s and 1970s and is expected to peak in 1983–84. Post-baccalaureate degree recipients in these areas are projected to continue growing relatively fast throughout the mid–1980s.

From now until 1985 the estimated number of business and management graduates each year will fall far short of projected openings. However, many recruiters regard a wide variety of college majors (for example, finance, accounting, business, economics, statistics, liberal arts) as substitute preparation for management employment, making it particularly difficult to predict shortages and surpluses.

There is a current debate over the possibility that the market for M.B.A.s will soon reach a saturation point.[18] Given their continuing increase and their high salaries relative to those with Bachelors' degrees in business and related fields, the conditions are ripe for such a result. If recruiters shift more of their demands toward the less-expensive Bachelor degree holders, in light of the much slower growth and projected decline at this level, these business-related undergraduates will be entering a much stronger market.

Accountants. The demand for accountants has been fairly strong and projections indicate future demand will be slightly above average.[19] This favorable job market has enticed students to enter this field; the result has been a threefold increase of Bachelor degree recipients and a sixfold increase of Master degree recipients from 1960–61 to 1975–76. Annual job openings for accountants, however, still exceed the annual number of degrees awarded. If education and employment trends continue, by the mid-1980s this gap should close. But if, as appears to be the case, recruiters are seeking four-year college degree graduates for a growing number of accounting jobs, the market for these graduates will remain strong.

Teachers. Education graduates entered favorable job markets in the 1960s, but their counterparts in the 1970s, especially in the latter half of the decade, were not so lucky. The depressed labor market for teachers was brought on primarily by the declining school-age population. These demographic changes were felt in elementary schools in the early 1970s, then in secondary schools in the late 1970s. Although the population is again increasing as the 1950s "baby boom" cohort has reached child-bearing age, employment prospects for teachers are expected to remain depressed through the mid–1980s.

The output of Bachelor degrees in education is expected to fall rapidly during the 1980s, but surpluses are still expected. Job openings will exist because of replacement needs but competition for these positions will be stiff. Masters and Doctor's degrees in education should keep growing throughout the mid-1980s, thus further intensifying the surpluses.

Graduate-level degrees in education accounted for fewer than half of the degrees conferred in education in 1975–76, but they are projected to account for almost two thirds by 1986–87.[20] Given this change in the composition of the available relevant labor supply, when the market for teachers picks up again in the late 1980s and 1990s, employers may insist that teachers have a graduate degree for entry-level positions.

Health professions. Employment demand for professional medical and other health workers increased rapidly during the 1960s and 1970s and is projected to grow faster than average through the mid–1980s.

Registered nurses are expected to enter a very favorable job market through the mid–1980s, as average annual openings far surpass the projected educational output.[21] In addition, job openings for licensed practical nurses, physicians, therapists, and rehabilitation occupations are expected to exceed health-trained labor force entrants. Health service administration, which usually requires a Master's degree, is expected to grow 45 percent from 1976 to 1985, but vacancies will exceed new graduates by a ratio of more than 5 to 1.[22] To meet this growth, employers will have to utilize nonhealth administration specialists.

STARTING SALARIES

In addition to examining projected imbalances in the labor market, it is also important to analyze salary patterns. Changes in pay can be even more important as an influence upon enrollment patterns. Table 11 shows national salary offers made to Bachelor degree recipients between 1973–74 and 1979–80. Engineering and computer science graduates were offered relatively high salaries throughout this period. Salaries of health degree recipients were above average and experienced relatively fast growth relative to the humanities, social sciences, and marketing graduates. Starting offers for graduates with accounting degrees remained above those for graduates in the social sciences, humanities, and business fields; however, they rose more slowly.

Table 12 shows that there was much less variation in starting salaries and recent salary increases for Master's degree candidates.[23] Salary offers for engineering and computer science degree candidates again were relatively high and rose faster than those of other Master's candidates. M.B.A.s with technical undergraduate degrees were not only offered higher salaries than their counterparts with nontechnical undergraduate degrees, but also had salary offers increase faster over this period. M.B.A.s commanded high salary premiums over graduates with Bachelors' degrees in business administration.

From this salary data it appears that pay and enrollment adjustments are working as expected in response to changing patterns of demand. Although comparable data are not available for states or regions, fragmentary data and anecdotes suggest that similar processes are at work in New England. It appears that larger employers operate in a national market for highly educated labor, pay decisions are governed by nationwide competition for students, and starting salaries correspond roughly to the going rate nationally.

Despite this apparent correspondence between national and regional labor markets, there remains the possibility of some labor market difficulties of special concern to New England. For example, the previous characterization of the national labor market may not hold for smaller employers who operate from more regional sources of labor. Differentials in living costs and in the quality of life may also modify the competitiveness of salaries in New England. Moreover, market share may need to be considered. If New England's market share should decline because of lower industry demand, some decline in their pay com-

TABLE 11. National Average Monthly Salary Offers to Bachelor Degree Candidates (1973/74–1979/80)

Curriculum	Average Dollar Offers		Average Annual Percentage of Change		
	1973–74	1979–80	1973–74 to 1979–80	1973–74 to 1976–77	1977–78 to 1979–80
Business					
Accounting	925	1,293	+6.6	+4.9	+7.5
Business–general (including management)	803	1,218	+8.6	+5.1	+11.4
Marketing and distribution	769	1,145	+8.2	+5.5	+9.7
Humanities and social sciences					
Humanities	691	1,074	+9.2	+5.7	+11.7
Economics	—	1,252	—	—	+11.5
Social sciences[a]	737	1,072	+7.6	+5.7	+10.0
Engineering					
Engineering–aeronautical	961	1,648	+11.9	+9.2	+10.9
Engineering–chemical	1,042	1,801	+12.1	+11.1	+9.5
Engineering–civil	967	1,554	+10.1	+7.5	+10.4
Engineering–electrical	986	1,690	+11.9	+8.8	+11.8
Engineering–industrial	979	1,655	+11.5	+9.5	+10.6
Engineering–mechanical	1,001	1,703	+11.7	+9.5	+10.7
Engineering–metallurgical	1,004	1,726	+12.0	+10.3	+10.9
Engineering–mining	—	1,734	—	—	+7.9
Engineering–nuclear	—	1,668	—	—	+11.3
Engineering–petroleum	—	1,987	—	—	+10.1
Engineering–technology	934	1,585	+11.6	+8.7	+11.5

TABLE 11. *(continued)*

Curriculum	Average Dollar Offers		Average Annual Percentage of Change		
	1973–74	1979–80	1973–74 to 1979–80	1973–74 to 1976–77	1977–78 to 1979–80
Sciences					
Agricultural sciences	785	1,192	+8.6	+5.9	+11.8
Biological sciences	720	1,159	+10.2	+7.5	+6.0
Chemistry	884	1,459	+10.8	+8.2	+11.3
Computer science	915	1,558	+11.7	+7.6	+11.6
Health (medical) professions	733	1,153	+9.6	+7.3	+10.9
Mathematics	874	1,475	+11.5	+7.6	+12.3
Other physical and earth sciences	895	1,543	+12.1	+6.4	+12.3

[a]From 1976–77 Social Science category; does not include Economics.

Source: College Placement Council, Inc., *A Study of Beginning Offers* (Copyright © by the College Placement Council, Inc., Bethlehem, Pa., all rights reserved).

TABLE 12. National Average Monthly Salary Offers to Inexperienced[a] Masters' Degree candidates (1973/74–1979/80)

Graduate Program	Average Dollar Offers		Average Annual Percentage of Change		
	1973–74	1979–80	1973–74 to 1979–80	1973–74 to 1976–77	1977–78 to 1979–80
Business administration–industrial					
Management or commerce[b]					
After nontechnical undergraduate degrees	1,181	1,795	+8.7	+6.5	+9.9
After technical undergraduate degree	1,235	1,171	+9.9	+7.2	+10.9
Accounting	—	1,873	—	—	+7.0
Humanities and social sciences					
Humanities	855	1,309	+8.9	+5.8	+15.0
Social science	917	1,298	+6.9	+4.3	+8.9
Engineering					
Chemical	1,172	1,947	+11.0	+9.6	+9.8
Civil	1,102	1,753	+9.9	+7.3	+9.9
Electrical	1,149	1,912	+11.1	+7.6	+11.4
Industrial	1,120	1,861	+11.0	+8.7	+11.2
Mechanical	1,138	1,893	+11.1	+8.8	+10.3
Nuclear	—	1,831	—	—	+11.9
Physics	1,089	—	—	—	—
Sciences					
Agriculture and related sciences	950	—	—	—	—
Chemistry	1,050	1,688	+10.1	+8.6	+5.7
Computer science	1,120	1,858	+11.0	+7.7	+10.3

TABLE 12. *(continued)*

Graduate Program	Average Dollar Offers		Average Annual Percentage of Change		
	1973–74	1979–80	1973–74 to 1979–80	1973–74 to 1976–77	1977–78 to 1979–80
Sciences					
Mathematics	1,042	1,685	+10.3	+7.8	+9.5
Metallurgy	1,131	1,891	+11.2	+8.1	+10.5
Geology and related geological sciences	—	1,873	—	—	+11.8

[a]One year or less, fulltime, nonmilitary employment.

[b]1979–80 figures for M.B.A.s only.

Source: College Placement Council, Inc., *A Study of Beginning Offers* (Copyright © by the College Placement Council, Inc., Bethlehem, Pa., all rights reserved).

petitiveness could be tolerated. If it should increase, it will have to compete more aggressively for labor than in the past.

For the occupations examined earlier, the projected market-share situation is mixed. Because New England has had a larger share of its employment in engineering, computers, accounting, and health when compared to the country as a whole, it has been competing disproportionately in tight occupational markets characterized by shortages and relatively fast salary increases.

New England's market share of engineers and accountants is projected to decline slightly in the 1980s.[24] The New England share of computer specialists is expected to remain roughly stable. The region's market share of managers and administrators will increase, causing greater pressure in procuring business-trained graduates unless employers make adjustments. In short, the labor market situation as it relates to constraints on regional economic development is not expected to deteriorate substantially during the 1980s and may improve marginally in some previously scarce occupations.

ADJUSTMENTS WITHIN THE NEW ENGLAND HIGHER EDUCATION SYSTEM

The preceding discussion has argued that, with some notable exceptions, the higher-education sector does a reasonably good job of meeting demand conditions in the labor market, although often with a lag. The responsiveness of this sector, however, has been controlled largely by *students'* career choices, and these choices have contributed to periodic market imbalances.

Employers do not appear to play a direct role in shaping the pattern of enrollments, except through financial aid and research support. Instead, employers' staffing needs find expression through the labor market in the form of salary offers and job openings. Because enrollments, particularly in scientific and engineering fields, are sensitive to such market signals, higher education ends by being responsive to the shifting job structure of the economy.

The higher education sector, however, is not monolithic in its responsiveness. There are distinctions between public and private institutions, between two-year and four-year institutions, and between undergraduate and postgraduate programs. Furthermore, because some institutions operate in both teaching and research markets and others do not, the pattern of institutional responsiveness to the market for teaching will spill over into research capability.

INSTITUTIONAL STRUCTURE

The structure of the higher-education system in New England is somewhat distinct from that of the country as a whole. For example, private institutions play an unusually large role in New England (Table 13). Though less than one quarter of enrollments nationally were in privately controlled institutions in 1978, almost half of all New England enrollments were in private schools.

TABLE 13. Distribution of Enrollments and Institutions in Higher Education by Type of Institution and Control, New England Versus United States (1978)

	Enrollments Percentage Private		Institutions Percentage Private	
	New England	U.S.	New England	U.S.
All institutions	48.6	22.4	66.7	53.0
College and universities	56.3	25.6	36.4	59.4
Other four-year	58.7	36.4	75.2	74.5
Two-year	13.4	4.5	37.8	22.5

Sources: Andrew J. Pepin, National Center for Education Statistics, *Fall Enrollment in Higher Education, 1978* (Washington, D.C.: U.S. Government Printing Office, 1979), pp. 46–61.
W. Grant and L. J. Eiden, National Center for Education Statistics, *Digest of Education Statistics, 1980* (Washington, D.C.: U.S. Government Printing Office, 1980), p. 114.

Despite the importance of private higher education in New England, the public sector dominated the growth in enrollments during the 1960s and 1970s. At the beginning of the 1960s private sector enrollments accounted for three quarters of the region's enrollments, compared to less than half by 1978.[25] By degree level, professional degrees showed the greatest growth followed by Associate degrees. This growth lagged slightly behind that for the country as a whole.[26]

Growth in enrollment also brought growth in the number of schools. The number of institutions of higher education in New England rose from 189 in 1959 to 261 in 1978, the bulk of this growth taking place in the 1960s.[27] The growth brought substantial change in the institutional composition of higher education.

Definitions and reporting categories have been modified in the last twenty years, making exact comparisons over time difficult if not impossible. Basic trends emerge, however. For instance, the major growth area has been the two-year colleges, particularly those which are publicly controlled.

There was relatively little change in the total of four-year public and private colleges and universities in New England during these decades. This stability, however, masks considerable institutional turnover. Of the 31 institutions that closed in the region between 1968 and 1978, 24 were private four-year colleges.[28] No public four-year institution closed. Seven two-year colleges closed, 6 of which were privately controlled. In addition, 7 institutions of higher education in the region merged with other institutions between 1968 and 1978. Six of these seven were private, equally divided between two-year and four-year institutions.

Another source of institutional change took place *within* schools, as fifteen New England schools were reclassified during this period.[29] Twelve of the reclassifications involved two-year private institutions that became four-year private institutions. Two private four-year institutions changed to private two-year schools and one two-year college switched from public to private control. While the national trend was for private two-year colleges to close, in New England these schools were much more likely to evolve, via merger or internal reorganization, into four-year colleges.

How will this changing system of higher education in New England be affected by the enrollment changes of the 1980s? A review of national projections of higher-education enrollments to 1985 yield a wide range of future scenarios. The majority of studies foresee an overall decline in college enrollments in the 1980s of 8–9 percent annually in the first half of the decade, with smaller decreases through the latter half.[30] Pessimistic estimates foresee a decline in enrollments to one half their 1974 level as a result of a weakened job market for college graduates.[31] Optimistic projections, ranging from slight increases to a doubling or tripling of total enrollments, predict much higher attendance rates of part-time nontraditional students.[32]

Among forecasters of overall enrollment declines, there seems to be a consensus that the private schools, particularly the four-year institutions, will be affected.[33] The small, less-selective, sectarian, liberal arts colleges and the private two-year colleges appear most vulnerable, especially those which recruit locally or regionally. New England, unfortunately, has a disproportionately large number of schools in these categories. Assuming continued availability of public funds, two-year community colleges, selective liberal arts colleges, and universities are expected to do relatively well.

These trends—the move toward two-year public education, toward part-time enrollments, and toward vocationally useful programs—will be felt in the pattern of school closings and in the reallocation of faculty resources within schools.

Institutional change in the market for teaching will, in turn, have important implications for the second market for higher education services—research. Because the structure of the higher-education system is so strongly shaped by student enrollment trends, the shift from liberal arts and humanities to more vocational subjects, the pressure for survival placed on private higher education, and the shift to two-year programs all compound to weaken the region's research universities. Research universities with established programs cannot shift resources rapidly from field to field. Institutions that are growing, newer schools with fewer tenured faculty, those with programs that do not need expensive lab, classroom, or dormitory facilities, and those with short duration programs are much more able to adapt to changing patterns of student demand. Funds may simply not be available to support either the maintenance of research facilities or the faculty and graduate students needed to undertake new research. For these reasons, the overall responsiveness of the higher-education system to labor market developments may at the same time be undermining the region's university-based research capability.

RESPONSIVENESS OF THE HIGHER EDUCATION SECTOR TO RESEARCH NEEDS

Apart from providing educational services, universities and colleges also generate research and development. Since the work of Abramowitz and Solow in the 1950s, economists have come increasingly to realize the importance of research and development activity for economic growth. Simply put, scientific advances are an important contributor to increased productivity, which in turn is a significant element for improvement in the standard of living.

R & D PRODUCTIVITY GROWTH

Although there is widespread consensus among economists that research and development expenditures yield substantial economic benefits, measurement problems hamper agreement on the exact magnitude of these benefits. The simplest approach to measuring the contribution of R & D to growth is to account for gains in productivity in terms of measurable factors, such as growth in labor and capital, and to attribute the remainder to "advances in knowledge" (Table 14). This residual accounted for over 50 percent of national productivity growth during 1948–69 and 100 percent during 1969–73.[34] During the late 1970s, however, the growth rate in productivity measured in this way decreased.

Attempts to measure directly the effect of R & D spending on productivity have tended to be somewhat less general. Some have calculated rates of return at the industry level and found these to vary from about 30 to 50 percent.[35] Others have computed rates of returns to firms with estimates averaging between 17 and 19 percent (although in some industries the returns were considerably higher).[36]

TABLE 14. Sources of Growth of National Income per Person Employed Nonresidential Business Sector

Item	1948–69	1969–73	1973–76
Growth rate of NIPPE	2.6	1.6	–0.5
Effect of irregular factors	–0.1	–0.5	0.1
Adjusted growth rate	2.7	2.1	–0.6
Changes in labor characteristics			
Hours of work	–0.2	–0.3	–0.5
Age-Sex composition	–0.1	–0.4	–0.3
Education	0.5	0.7	0.9
Changes in capital and land per person employed:			
Structures and equipment	0.3	0.2	0.2
Inventories	0.1	0.1	0.0
Land	0.0	–0.1	0.0
Improved allocation of resources	0.4	0.1	0.0
Changes in legal and human environment	0.0	–0.2	–0.4
Economies of scale	0.4	0.4	0.2
Advances of knowledge (and not elsewhere classified)	1.4	1.6	–0.7

Source: E. Denison, *Accounting for Slower Economic Growth,* Washington, D.C.: The Brookings Institution, 1979).

Paralleling the trends in productivity, total real national expenditure on R & D through most of the 1970s has stayed below its peak of the late 1960s (Table 15). The reason for this reduction in the seventies was the cut in real federal R & D spending. The federal government supplied 62 percent of total R & D funds in 1967, but this proportion dropped to below 50 percent by 1979.

TABLE 15. Expenditures on Research and Development, United States, 1953–79

(billions of dollars)

Year	Total R & D Expenditures (current $)	Total R & D Expenditures (1972 $)	Industry R & D Expenditures (1972 $)	Government R & D Expenditures (1972 $)
1953	5.1	8.7	3.8	4.7
1955	6.2	10.1	4.1	5.8
1957	9.8	15.1	5.3	9.4
1959	12.4	18.3	6.0	11.9
1961	14.3	20.7	6.9	13.4
1963	17.1	23.9	7.6	15.7
1965	20.1	27.0	8.8	17.5
1967	23.2	29.4	10.3	18.2
1969	25.7	29.6	11.5	17.2
1971	26.7	27.9	11.3	15.6
1973	30.4	28.8	12.2	15.5
1975	35.2	27.7	12.1	14.6
1977	42.9	29.2	12.9	14.3
1979	52.4	32.0	15.1	15.8

Source: National Science Foundation, reproduced in E. Mansfield, "Technology and Productivity in the United States," National Bureau of Economic Research Conference Paper Series, No. 18, March 1980.

Looking at these figures, a natural conclusion is that the slowdown in productivity is due to the fall in real R & D spending, with the bulk of the blame resting squarely on the federal government.[37] On the other hand, it has been argued that it is not the slowdown in R & D spending that accounts for the fall in the growth of labor productivity since 1968; rather, a key factor seems to be that R & D has become extremely unproductive in this period.[38] If this is true, it raises the question of the pattern of federal R & D spending rather than just its size.

FEDERAL R & D AND UNIVERSITIES

It is useful to examine the structure of federal R & D spending in this context, particularly as it applied to universities and colleges. Universities are overshadowed by private industry. Businesses undertake the largest amount of all R & D, and of federally financed R & D as well. In 1976 over 50 percent of federal R & D funds went to industry; only 12.4 percent went to colleges and universities; with another 5.4 percent to university-administered federally funded R & D centers (FFRDCs) (Table 16). In a total university R & D budget of $3.7 billion, $2.5 billion (67.6 percent) came from the government, $800 million (21.6 percent) came from internal sources, while only $100 million (2.7 percent) came from industry. Thus the bulk of university research money comes from the government and other nonprofit sources.

This is consistent with the notion that universities tend to do more basic research than industry. Universities spend 46 percent of the allocation on basic research and another 42 percent on applied research; the corresponding industry figures are a mere 2 percent and 14 percent. Overall federal allocations to basic research grew slowly throughout the seventies, rising from 12.3 percent of the federal R & D budget in 1970 to 14.8 percent in 1980, but the share of colleges and universities rose from 9.6 percent in 1970 to 13.2 percent in 1980 (Tables 17 and 18).

The Department of Defense continues to be by far the leading support agency for R & D, but its relative share of the federal R & D pie has been declining—from 48 percent in 1970 to 43 percent in 1978. The three agencies whose relative share has grown the most in this period are the Environmental Protection Agency (from 0.6 percent to 1.5 percent), the Department of Energy (from 8.8 percent to 16.1 percent), and the Department of HEW (from 8 percent to 12.1 percent). The agency whose share has dropped the most is NASA (Table 19).

New England universities are particularly fortunate in their allocations of federal R & D money. They have received a relatively stable 9 percent share of total federal R & D grants throughout the 1970s while accounting for only 6.3 percent of all enrollments in higher education in the United States, and for 7.6 percent of graduate enrollments (Table 20). Thus higher education is an export industry in terms of research as well as students. Massachusetts has consistently received the third highest R & D allocations in the country, after California and New York. While Massachusetts accounts for only 54 percent of New England's students, the state receives 64 percent of New England's federal R & D

TABLE 16. Intersectoral Transfers of Funds for Research and Development, United States, 1976
(billions of dollars)

	Performers					
Sources of Funds	Federal Government	Industry	Universities and Colleges	FFRDC's	Other Nonprofit Institutions	Total
Federal government	5.6	10.2	2.5	1.1	0.8	20.2
Industry	—	16.3	0.1	—	0.1	16.5
Universities and college	—	—	0.8	—	—	0.8
Other nonprofit institutions	—	—	0.3	—	0.3	0.6
Total	5.6	26.5	3.7	1.1	1.2	38.1

Source: National Science Foundation, reproduced in E. Mansfield, "Technology and Productivity,"

TABLE 17. Federal Obligations for Research and Development by Character of Work: Fiscal Years 1970–1980

(millions of dollars)

Fiscal Year	Total	Research: Basic	Research: Applied	Development
1970	15,340	1,887 (12.3)[b]	3,064	10,389
1971	15,545	1,957 (12.6)	3,294	10,294
1972	16,498	2,179 (13.2)	3,414	10,905
1973	16,800	2,211 (13.2)	3,435	11,154
1974	17,415	2,365 (13.6)	3,855	11,195
1975	19,047	2,591 (13.6)	4,258	12,198
1976	20,789	2,759 (13.3)	4,865	13,165
1977	23,995	3,256 (13.6)	5,359	15,380
1978	26,414	3,699 (14.0)	6,052	16,663
1979[a]	29,576	4,205 (14.2)	6,684	18,687
1980[a]	30,733	4,538 (14.8)	7,056	19,140

[a]Estimates.

[b]Numbers in parentheses are percentages.

Source: National Science Foundation, *Federal Funds for Research and Development* (Washington, D.C.: U.S. Government Printing Office, 1980).

money (Table 21). The largest recipients of federal R & D funds in the region are M.I.T. (second nationally), Harvard (ninth nationally), Yale, Boston University, University of Massachusetts at Amherst, University of Connecticut, and Woods Hole Oceanographic Institute. In 1978 New England also received 5.9 percent of the $1.68 billion allocated to university-administered federal R & D centers (in this case, M.I.T.'s Lincoln Laboratory) and 20.4 percent of the $642 million granted to other nonprofit institutions (much of this going to the Draper Laboratory, formerly at M.I.T.).

TABLE 18. Federal Obligations for Research and Development by Performer Fiscal Years 1970 and 1979–80
(millions of dollars)

Performer	Actual 1970	1978	1979	Estimated 1980
Total	15,340	26,414	29,576	30,733
Federal intramural	4,018	6,882	7,521	7,747
Industrial firms	7,822	11,840	13,651	14,267
FFRDC's administered by industrial firms	431	1,242	1,255	1,269
Universities and colleges	1,473	3,400	3,864	4,048
FFRDC's administered by universities	751	1,326	1,411	1,500
Other nonprofit institutions	458	1,018	1,140	1,090
FFRDC's administered by nonprofit institutions	247	316	329	396
State and local governments	100	268	280	289
Foreign	40	153	124	127

Source: National Science Foundation, *Federal Funds for Research and Development* (Washington, D.C.: U.S. Government Printing Office, 1980).

Nationwide, private institutions account for only 22.4 percent of enrollments, but receive 39 percent of the R & D grants. This weighting toward private institutions carries over in New England also, where private institutions have 48.6 percent of enrollments and 73.2 percent of the federal R & D allocations (Table 22).

In sum, New England receives a major share of federal R & D allocations, thanks to the region's many fine education institutions. There is no doubt that the region receives the direct benefit of these expenditures. Less obvious but also clearly present are the many indirect benefits that accrue to the region. In particular, as a consequence of the large concentration of funds at M.I.T., a significant electronics industry has developed around Boston.[39] More recently, with the shift in emphasis toward energy and health, casual observation seems to indicate that there are newly emerging concentrations of energy-related and medical-technology companies in the area. These indirect spillovers of federal R & D spending probably have a much larger long-run economic impact than the expenditures themselves, and therefore deserve to be considered in somewhat greater detail.

TABLE 19. Federal R & D Obligations by Leading Support Agency: Fiscal Years 1970–78 (millions of dollars)

Agency	1970	1971	1972	1973	1974	1975	1976	1977	1978	Av. Annual % Change 1970–1978
Total, all agencies	15,340.3	15,545.0	16,497.8	16,800.1	17,414.7	19,047.1	20,788.9	23,995.0	26,414.3	+7.0
Department of Defense	7,360.4	7,509.0	8,318.1	8,404.2	8,420.4	9,012.5	9,654.7	10,963.4	11,553.6	+5.8
Total, all agencies Minus DOD	7,979.9	8,036.0	8,179.6	8,395.9	8,994.3	10,034.6	11,134.2	13,031.6	14,860.6	+8.1
Department of Energy	1,341.0	1,302.9	1,297.7	1,363.2	1,488.9	2,047.3	2,463.8	3,536.2	4,244.8	+15.4
NASA	3,799.9	3,257.9	3,157.2	3,060.9	3,002.2	3,064.4	3,446.8	3,703.4	3,875.4	+1.1
HEW	1,221.0	1,476.1	1,751.1	1,837.6	2,290.1	2,397.5	2,583.6	2,823.3	3,207.3	+12.8
NSF	289.0	336.9	454.8	479.9	556.4	595.0	609.3	697.0	748.8	+12.6
Department of Agriculture	281.2	304.9	349.6	366.5	378.7	420.1	462.4	547.0	621.3	+10.4
Environmental Protection Agency	88.5	136.7	122.4	180.6	169.2	257.7	259.1	295.5	384.6	+19.5
Department of Interior	157.9	193.7	220.3	243.4	196.6	311.2	342.0	326.1	385.2	+11.8
Department of Transportation	327.8	497.2	310.5	310.6	369.8	311.6	294.5	354.6	408.3	+2.5
Department of Commerce	121.6	143.7	187.3	190.6	180.6	215.4	228.9	244.7	283.7	+11.2
All others	347.1	385.8	328.8	362.6	361.8	414.6	443.8	503.8	701.3	+9.2

Source: National Science Foundation, *Federal Funds for Research and Development* (Washington, D.C.: U.S. Government Printing Office, 1980).

TABLE 20. Federal Obligations to Universities and Colleges by Geographical Division and States Fiscal Years 1971–78 (thousands of dollars)

	1971	1972	1973	1974	1975	1976	1977	1978
United States, total	3,498,596	4,144,570	3,838,919	4,480,169	4,547,075	5,402,506	6,486,103	7,479,177
New England, total	348,556	418,516	403,097	397,431	417,449	470,718	580,619	673,576
Connecticut	57,182	69,697	62,809	80,189	76,159	84,859	101,262	115,839
Maine	6,832	8,877	11,077	9,921	16,520	21,972	23,893	28,439
Massachusetts	238,776	288,183	281,024	255,810	261,968	289,431	367,233	430,892
New Hampshire	19,357	16,652	14,623	16,068	17,411	21,925	28,624	29,910
Rhode Island	16,188	21,671	21,399	21,273	24,901	29,896	34,191	37,776
Vermont	10,221	13,436	12,165	14,170	20,490	22,535	25,416	30,720

Source: National Science Foundation, *Federal Support to Universities, Colleges, and Selected Nonprofit Institutions, Fiscal Year, 1978* (Washington, D.C.: U.S. Government Printing Office, 1980).

TABLE 21. Federal R & D and Student Enrollment in New England, by State (fiscal year 1978)

	Federal R & D (000's)	%	Student Enrollment	%	Federal R & D Per Student
Connecticut	115,839	17.2	152,431	21.4	759.9
Maine	28,439	4.2	41,460	5.8	685.9
Massachusetts	430,892	64.0	384,500	53.9	1,120.7
New Hampshire	29,910	4.4	41,549	5.8	719.9
Rhode Island	37,776	5.6	63,553	3.9	594.4
Vermont	30,720	4.6	29,577	4.1	1,038.6
New England	673,576	100.0	713,070	99.9	944.6

Sources: National Science Foundation, *Federal Support to Universities, Colleges, and Selected Nonprofit Institutions, Fiscal Year, 1978* (Washington, D.C.: U.S. Government Printing Office, 1980).

Digest of Education Statistics, 1980, National Center for Education Statistics, p. 83.

MODELS OF R & D IN INSTITUTIONS OF HIGHER EDUCATION

Research and economic growth are linked through the process of utilization of research results. New England's universities engage in both research and transfer of results to potential users.

Models of research and dissemination or diffusion of results vary somewhat from field to field. The agricultural model is highly touted as the most comprehensive. It is a decentralized system that operates in every state and county in the United States. It was initiated as a result of the enactment of the Morrill Act of 1862, which established land grant universities. Each such university was mandated to maintain an agricultural experiment station and to conduct agricultural research.

Later it became clear that benefits from agricultural research were increased when farmers used the research results. Farmers were likely to use results that increased productivity or solved farm-management problems.

In 1914 the Smith-Lever Act authorized the agricultural Extension Service. The purpose of the service was to give, through the land grant universities, "instruction and practical demonstration in agriculture and home economics and related subjects and to encourage the application of such information by means of demonstrations, publications, and otherwise to persons not attending or resident in the colleges." The Extension Service was thus created as the complement to agricultural re-

TABLE 22. Federal R & D in Universities by State and Type of Control: FY 1978

(thousands of dollars)

	Public Institutions		Private Institutions	
	Spending	%	Spending	%
United States	4,565,111	61.0	2,914,066	39.0
New England	180,404	26.8	493,172	73.2
Connecticut	35,486	30.6	80,353	69.4
Maine	23,004	80.9	5,435	19.1
Massachusetts	64,929	15.1	365,963	84.9
New Hampshire	14,825	49.6	15,085	50.4
Rhode Island	17,011	45.0	20,765	55.0
Vermont	25,149	81.9	5,571	18.1

Source: National Science Foundation, *Federal Support to Universities, Colleges, and Selected Nonprofit Institutions, Fiscal Year, 1978* (Washington, D.C.: U.S. Government Printing Office, 1980).

search. In addition to basic research, applied research could be conducted in response to needs expressed by farmers to Extension Service agents. The "system" was based on a two-way communication loop between researchers and research users.

Attempts have been made to adapt the agricultural model to other fields, but to date none of these efforts has been as succesful.[40] As a result, in fields other than agriculture both research and dissemination of results are conducted in a less systematic fashion, and no institutionalized mechanism for diffusion and feedback exists.

In science and engineering, research is to a larger degree centralized in research centers. In part this may be because of the cost of facilities and equipment and also because the fields tend to be more specialized. Since both the scientific and user communities are relatively concentrated, the need for dissemination of results to a large audience is almost nonexistent. Whether broader diffusion of results among the scientific communities would stimulate more or better research is not clear, and there may be dissemination problems related to patents and proprietary research information.

Research and dissemination in the biomedical and health fields has aspects of both the agricultural and science and engineering models. Biomedical research needs are subject to less local or regional variation than agricultural requirements and often require expensive facilities. Thus large research centers have developed which focus on different health problems. At the same time, the results of research can be used not only by other researchers, but also by clinicians throughout the country. Therefore, there is a vast network for dissemination of results through continuing education, journals, conferences, and professional societies.

Business-related research tends to be less theoretical and more applied. There are no major research centers, no comprehensive systems, and no national networks for communication of results. Research is often directed to the needs of particular situations, although it involves application of more generalized tools. Results are often directly provided to the research user by faculty members through consultation and technical assistance to companies. In contrast, economic research tends to be more theoretical; results that can be directly applied by the practitioner are not usual except in program evaluation and forecasting. Potential users of results are not often identified. Diffusion of results is primarily among economists.

Research in public policy and government is a relatively new phenomenon, and the structure for dissemination of results is evolving. Most research is of the applied type, by virtue of the definition of the field itself. It might be assumed that public policy research follows the lines of agricultural research. Although the federal government is a highly concentrated consumer of policy research, many programs, as well as state and municipal governments, are decentralized. To date, however, public policy research appears to partake of the weaknesses of both business and economic research.

These general approaches to R & D are manifested in New England in a variety of ways. Each state in New England has a land grant university and an associated agriculture experiment station and Extension Service. New England's universities have notable science and engineering research programs. M.I.T.'s Industrial Liaison Program is unique in its research/user linkage structure.

A considerable amount of the nation's clinical, health policy, and health education research is conducted in New England at medical schools and also at research centers like M.I.T.'s Arteriosclerosis Center and the University of Vermont's Regional Cancer Center. There are many examples of research on the problems of business and on issues of regional economic development. There is the Center for Research on

Business and Economics at the University of Rhode Island; Harvard and M.I.T. have housed the largest group of Nobel laureates in Economics; Boston College, the University of Massachusetts, the Harvard Business School, Bentley College, and Babson College have all been active in small business assistance.

TECHNOLOGY SPIN–OFFS

A final issue in research and research implementation is the commercialization of R & D. It is widely believed that higher education makes an important indirect contribution to the commercialization of R & D and that the creation and growth of certain types of industry is often ultimately linked to a university. The primary examples are the complex of industry along Route 128 outside Boston, alleged to be directly tied to M.I.T., and the burgeoning industrial activity of Santa Clara county in California, said to owe its growth to Stanford.

In principle this so-called transfer of technology could take place in two ways. One possibility would be for an existing company to buy or otherwise acquire a bit of knowledge (say blueprints for a new product) and then to commercialize it. Alternatively, the person or persons responsible for the idea or design could develop it into a marketable product, either within an existing organization or by forming a new company.

It appears that the former process is relatively rare. It is generally thought that for an innovation to be successful, it needs a champion, and the most obvious candidate is the inventor. Particularly in the case of sophisticated technologies at the frontier of research, it is difficult for someone relatively unfamiliar with the design of the product to commercialize it efficiently. One famous example is a new computer design that was publicly available (since it had been produced under a government contract at M.I.T.). Only the original designers had the know-how to develop it, however, so they set up their own company, Digital Equipment Corporation.

More generally, the most common vehicle for the commercialization of R & D generated at M.I.T. has been the new venture. A series of studies on the formation of new companies by former M.I.T. personnel found that by 1968 a total of at least 165 new companies had spun off government-sponsored research programs at various M.I.T. laboratories and academic departments.[41] This by itself is an impressive number and seems to lend credence to the notion that the industrialization of Route 128 was closely related to university research.

To what extent was the generation of spin-offs something unique at M.I.T.? Are there factors specific to a university that particularly encourage the development and then diffusion of new technology? A study of several independent, technology-oriented research organizations showed similar patterns of spin-offs.[42] Although precise figures on the number of spin-offs per million dollars of government R & D funds are not available, the basic point seems to be clear—that universities do not have a monopoly on developing new technologies and spinning off companies to exploit them. These other organizations, however, were closely related to M.I.T. and there is no guarantee that they will persist in spinning off new firms the way M.I.T. can and has. The continual generation of new ideas probably depends a great deal on a milieu of fundamental research.

Apart from the number of spin-off companies, it should be noted that within a few years of the big jump in government-research expenditures, the spin-offs from the three largest M.I.T. laboratories (a total of 94 firms) accounted for more jobs than the originating laboratories. Sales grew exponentially, and in fact the success rate was 80 percent, as compared to a nationwide figure of 50 percent.

This succes was due to the particular nature of these new ventures and the relationship of their founders with the government. An examination of the nature of their business shows that a large proportion of the firms in their initial years relied considerably on consulting and contract R & D work for the government. Thus during the critical start-up years when most companies falter because of low demand, the technology-based companies around M.I.T. were able to rely on the contacts of their founders to obtain contract work. Over time this reliance on the provision of services gradually declined, to be replaced largely by production of hardware. The main customer, however, continued to be the government. On average for these firms, only about 30 percent of their sales were to the nongovernment sector. And this figure remained roughly stable over time.

OPTIONS FOR THE FUTURE

This survey of the role and prospects for higher education in the New England economy has examined the two markets for higher education services—the labor market and the R & D market. From the point of view of higher education, the 1980s are likely to be years of recession in both markets unless circumstances change in unanticipated ways.

From the perspective of the economy, however, the situation is more complex. Higher education has generally served the economy well as a provider of skills. For certain fields, like engineering, however, the traditional response mechanisms have not worked nearly so well—producing surpluses in some periods and shortages in others. In particular, for engineers and scientists the shortages of the late 1970s will reach, in varying degrees, into the 1980s. Barring some major shift in demand, however, balanced labor markets are likely to be achieved in New England by the late 1980s. In the R & D market the historical record of performance has been much better than the recent experience.

The causes of weak performance in the labor market are inherent in the responsiveness of the educational system to enrollment shifts and student career decisions. As long as higher education remains highly sensitive to enrollments, imbalances are likely to occur. By its nature, R & D prospects and performance are much more difficult to predict than those of the labor market. There are, however, some structural deficiencies in the conduct and implementation of research described earlier which deserve policy action.

In terms of improving the economic performance of higher education, the current decade is too short a period to accomplish more than quick-fix improvements in the system. Projections for the late 1990s indicate that the decline in the college-age population will have reversed, and this should speed a return to the historical postwar levels of enrollments. Moreover, it will be time to utilize the R & D of the 1980s.

Given these conditions, it is appropriate to ask not only how well will higher education serve the skill needs of the economy in the 1980s, but what structure should it retain once the shake-out of the 1980s has been accomplished? For the educational recovery of the 1990s, what should be the mix of public and private institutions? How much and where should research capability exist? How much education and what type should be available?

SHORT–TERM CHANGES IN HIGHER EDUCATION PROGRAMS

In the immediate future, the principal changes with regard to the functioning of the labor market involve accelerating flows of students into shortage occupations and avoiding subsequent surpluses. These changes center on improved planning, program flexibility, and the provision of services to nontraditional students. By now they are part of the conventional wisdom about how higher education should be preparing for the 1980s.

The problems of limited skill scarcities hampering economic development in New England should be largely resolved by enrollment and institutional change in the 1980s. Declines in research and research capability during the 1980s, however, may create new problems for growth in the 1990s.

Student advising and counseling should reflect better information about employment gaps, in order to spot conditions leading to gluts and in order to anticipate shortages in areas where adjustment lags are significant. This will require better planning data, such as market-wide estimates of employment gaps and closer monitoring of employers' staffing trends and of enrollments by field to fine-tune the management of skill supplies.

Similar planning information should be factored into faculty appointments and facilities planning. The higher education sector must maintain a precarious balance between having the teaching capacity to meet peak demands of the economy and avoiding longer commitments to faculty or new facilities than can be supported by labor market demand. Fortunately, differences in the mix of tenure among institutions and the availability of underutilized educational plant allow for more system-wide flexibility than is possible within individual schools. Even where facilities and faculty are a system-wide constraint, adjunct faculty and private sector training and laboratory facilities offer a potential pool of educational resources. Drawing upon such opportunities, however, requires a harmonization among schools and the building of new relationships with the business sector.

Continuing education is often seen as a substitute for expected declines in the traditional student body in the 1980s. In terms of the labor market, however, continuing education is an avenue for accelerating the closure of the manpower gap by drawing upon those already employed and upon the growing pool of students in two-year college programs who are potential candidates for part-time baccalaureate programs as the college labor market recovers.

PLANNING FOR THE STRUCTURE OF THE HIGHER EDUCATION SECTOR

Over the longer term it is important to address questions of balance within the higher-education sector. The mix among types of institutions can have important implications for both teaching and research.

During the past two decades the structure has changed in uneven but significant ways. Schools have closed, opened, merged, and entered new markets. Public higher education has prospered, particularly at the level of two-year colleges. The private sector has held its own, although turnover has been substantial. What is needed for the 1980s, however, is a policy of systematic planning for teaching and research capacity to determine where needs exist and how they can be most effectively met. Before any new capacity is added to this sector, the possibility of interschool consortia and mergers should be fully explored. Faculty and student exchanges and transfers of existing physical facilities can more immediately overcome educational bottlenecks than any growth program based upon new capital expenditures and faculty recruitment.

MAINTAINING AND IMPROVING RESEARCH AND DEVELOPMENT CAPABILITY IN THE HIGHER EDUCATION SECTOR

The higher education sector has traditionally carried a major responsibility for basic research. While there is no indication of a diminished need for such research, the real amount of support in this area has been declining.

Higher education has been relatively less important in applied research and in research application. With some exceptions—agriculture research and some examples in engineering—the institutional capability to conduct and implement applied research is not well developed. The importance of applied research following the model of agricultural research and extension has been understood, but funding of this model has more often than not been neglected. Declining real resources and deficiencies in institutional capability may signal longer-term problems for economic development.

For example, when higher education is asked to provide research solutions to immediate problems of business and government, it often lacks both the backup of basic research needed to provide such answers and the familiarity with research utilization needed to provide useful results. Whether the problem is one of energy development, auto emissions, hospital cost control, or inflation, having a reserve of basic know-how is as important as having a reserve of trained personnel to utilize research. Addressing these problems requires adjustments in the mix as well as the level of R & D support.

Research also needs to be financed in a manner and at a level which allows it to compete more effectively with enrollments in shaping the structure of higher education. Enrollments are expected to shift from private to public institutions, yet five of the seven largest recipients of R & D resources in the region are private universities. Apart from agricultural research (where state universities have a virtual monopoly over federal funds), the importance of private higher education to research is even more evident. In planning for educational structure, the existing capability needs to be maintained, independent of trends in enrollments.

Finally, the pool of venture funding for R & D deserves consideration. If the investment analogy, already applied to education and product-oriented R & D, is extended further, it should be apparent that some research is risky in terms of the probability of paying off. Although some risky research can be judged by the usual tests of economic payoff, research that leads uncertainly to important scientific breakthroughs may deserve less restrictive support criteria. Universities have traditionally housed and supported this type of research. As financial stringencies increase, however, the scope for such discretionary support will inevitably narrow.

PROPRIETARY HIGHER EDUCATION

If these various financing objectives for R & D are to be met, traditional funding sources are not likely to be adequate. What alternatives are available?

If one purpose of expanding R & D is to increase the flow of commercially viable technologies and products, then business should invest in education-based research capability and receive a proportionate share of the benefits. Business philanthropy, of this sort has been limited in the past, however, and there is little sign of a major shift in the future.

A second possibility is for higher education to participate more aggressively in the markets for teaching, research, and application. For a variety of reasons, existing institutions in the higher-education sector cannot and should not respond fully to the shifting needs of the economy. The rapid identification of new educational markets, the speedy development of new curricula, and the ability to reallocate resources and to expand and contract faculty on short notice are not the strong points of institutions used to longer-term and more diverse objectives. Substantial programs of basic research cannot be undertaken as short-term commitments; teaching is built around long-duration degree-granting programs; laboratory facilities cannot be built overnight; and state legislatures are not likely to provide the budgetary flexibility needed to underwrite such responsiveness.

Similar observations have been made about postsecondary vocational education. But although the vocational education sector shares many of the sources of rigidity and conservatism found in the higher-education sector, post secondary *proprietary* schools are a source of much growth and dynamism. The quality of these schools is uneven, but the best provide models of responsiveness to, and effective relationships with, employers and markets. They move in and out of training fields with the ebb and flow of demand, meeting training needs not anticipated by, or responded to by, public and other not-for-profit schools.

Similarly, if R & D can be expected to yield substantial economic returns, a fair share of those returns could be returned to the research system through either equity investments or direct business participation. This would, in effect, institutionalize within the higher-education sector the business spin-offs launched by individual faculty.

To achieve the benefits of such entrepreneurial behavior and resource flexibility, consideration should be given to chartering proprietary institutions of higher education. These institutions could be a source of educational innovation, a mechanism for responding to short-term training needs of employers that are not met elsewhere in the system, a resource for R & D diffusion, and a way of generating new funds for R & D. These proprietary schools of higher education would be expected to meet the same standards of educational performance as not-for-profit schools, and would also have to meet market tests of profitability. They could be independent, as is the case in the postsecondary sector, or they could be affiliated with existing colleges and universities. Although such commercialization of higher education may pose important conflicts with other university goals and values, the trade-offs deserve explicit consideration.

REVERSING BUSINESS NEGLECT

There has been a recent wave of concern about and lobbying of higher education by business. Much of this effort has come from high-technology companies and has focused on the problem of persistent engineering shortages.

This attention has been somewhat unfortunate in that it has obscured longer-term issues of how higher education responds to economic change. Because higher education has generally operated effectively in both the labor market and the R & D market, there has been little incentive for business involvement in educational policy, except in time of acute scarcity. Moreover, higher education has long cherished its autonomy from economic and political influence and has not sought active business participation in its affairs. In the 1980s however, the economic concerns of business coincide unusually with those of higher education, thereby providing both the opportunity and the incentive to forge a closer relationship in the future.

4. THE UNIVERSITY'S CONTRIBUTION TO COMMUNITY ECONOMIC DEVELOPMENT: FIVE CASE STUDIES

Charles J. Stokes

In the nineteenth century it was an article of faith that the surest way to get a community growing was to establish a college there. Our history records long struggles over the location of state institutions, presumably resulting from such a belief. In this chapter we examine interactions. In what way does the university affect the economic development of its locale—a city, town, metro region, or geographical area?

Five models of such interaction will be examined: Stanford University and the San Mateo-Santa Clara County areas, the University of Chicago and the Hyde Park–Kenwood neighborhoods in Chicago, the Research Triangle in the Piedmont of North Carolina, the University of Colorado and the Boulder-Denver Corridor, and the University of Michigan and the Plymouth Road Corridor into Detroit. Each has been selected to illustrate a particular kind of interaction, but in no sense is this a full or complete sample of what the patterns of interaction can be or have been in the United States.

REGIONAL ECONOMIC DEVELOPMENT

Economic development is the alteration of the economic structure of a region so as to increase productivity and incomes. Higher incomes imply more jobs for more people. What is at issue is the capacity of the economy to generate and sustain annual increases in total production and income at levels that exceed the expected growth of the population.

A region that cannot develop a base for growth is one in which the standard of living must fall, either absolutely or relatively. In such a region a growing proportion of its population develops low morale and a sense that life there is not worthwhile. The percentage of people without the essentials of a decent standard of living grows. Development, then, is more than numbers. It is the *way* people develop. It is as much a state of mind as an economic and physical reality.

Thus the objectives of development are:

to increase the availability and widen the distribution of goods and services that sustain a decent life

to raise the quality of life so that a higher sense of personal worth is possible for larger and larger proportions of the population

to expand the range of choices—for jobs, for styles of living, for personal advancement—and reduce the limiting effects of poverty

In this context we searched for models. We have chosen examples of interaction which have produced more goods, more services, more jobs, more self esteem, more economic freedom, and much less poverty—a tall order, given the accepted purpose of a university but, as some see it, not an unreasonable one.

THE UNIVERSITY AND REGIONAL ECONOMIC DEVELOPMENT

Kenneth Schneider in his critique of the unkind traditions of urban society has said that "if the university in America early took a clear responsibility to create a society founded on... the agricultural and mechanical arts, its responsibility clearly now resides in adapting the vast human capacities for human benefits."[1] As Schneider sees it, the university's challenge is in four related efforts:

(a) to discover and develop a vital pertinence in teaching, research, and service that will parallel their critical engagement in the economic development of the nineteenth century

(b) to bring to bear all fields of knowledge on the region, the city, and the economy, as an articulate whole

(c) to make human values and goals consciously and directly a part of the concepts, analyses, research, and experimentation in all developmental questions

(d) to work out a tradition of organic wholeness and therefore human freedom as the university (its campus, its varied institutions, its faculty and its students) moves increasingly to the center stage

Regional development has four facets—the use of natural resources, the use of human resources, the use of technology, and the use of institutions. Natural resources while important can be overstressed. The quality and productivity of human beings is vital but is clearly dependent on technology and education, a vital institution. Perhaps education is the most essential of these facets. Particularly, the effect of a university collaborating with industry can play a large part in the development of technology.

THE CHICAGO MODEL

Howard Ray Rowland of St. Cloud State University of Minnesota has said, correctly, that there are four fundamental ways a college or university can and "should be involved with its community."[2] It can be a source of ideas and of information; it can be a service agency; and it can be a model or an example. The University of Chicago in Hyde Park–Kenwood is all of these and more. It is located on an urban island, in a vast sea of decay. Hyde Park–Kenwood is essentially a succès d'estime. There is no doubt that the University authorities found it necessary to assist as much as possible in the preservation of the middle-class atmosphere and values of this urban island, and thus of the university itself. Columbia, New York University, Harvard, Boston University, St. Louis University, Case Western Reserve, and Fordham among others are located in such urban islands, but in no case has the success in neighborhood preservation been as great as that in Chicago.

Four elements seem to explain the Chicago success. One clearly is the careful organization of neighborhood groups under competent leadership. It is hard to say how much of a role the university played in that element, but it was important. The second element is the clever and effective use of state and federal urban renewal funds. Here the university's role was essential, since it provided the seed money, the professional talent, and the sense of direction. The third element is the high quality of the basic housing and urban setting. Near Lake Michigan, served by a high quality electric suburban railway and fronted by magnificently designed parklands and laced by parkways, Hyde Park–Kenwood has been fortunate to have had a builder of great architectural talent. Few American urban neighborhoods have such a range of first-rate architecture and so little clutter. There was not much to redevelop, and what needed to be preserved was in good condition. Given half a chance, market values of the land and buildings could readily be preserved.

The last element is the absence of political conflict. Political leadership was positive, supportive, and distinctive. There were no confrontations between one group and another. Blacks and whites, both middle class and conservative, wanted to keep the area the same attractive place to live that it had been from the start. The difference in race was a footnote, but there had to be a willingness on the part of the middle-class whites to accept the views of middle-class blacks and be willing to live in the same neighborhood with them. Certainly, academics are more likely to accept membership to their group on ability rather than appearance.

Which of these four elements was most important at that time? The answer is not easy, since without the timing and the nature of the pace of preservation and redevelopment, any answer would be deceiving. The point is that all elements tended to meld and to play their relative roles at the proper time and in the necessary sequence.

Hyde Park–Kenwood is a microcosm of the best in Chicago. Along the Lake, highrise luxury apartments, some of them erected recently, are statements of the American way to reach the top. Along Greenwood, Kenwood, and University streets, the very wealthy built their mansions in styles reminiscent of the best of Europe and set them well back from the quiet, tree-shaded roads. Townhouses are the basic elements of the neighborhood, ranging from the familiar London Georgian to simple brownstones but including every style likely to be found in Eastern cities, showing that styles were varied to avoid monotony.

But the Chicago-style three-story apartment house found almost nowhere else in America is what is different about Hyde Park–Kenwood. Everywhere it is clear that this is a neighborhood meant to be enjoyed as an urban enclave.

By the 1950s, however, the wave of urban blight that had swept south from the Loop was threatening to engulf this enclave. It was not simply that poor black families in their search for better housing were moving into the precincts of a neighborhood that wanted to remain middle class. It was that without organized effort there was no way to stop a natural market reaction to changes in values. The University of Chicago despite its vast wealth was in no position to buy up Hyde Park–Kenwood. But it was in a position to cooperate, provide leadership, and even help to finance some of the key elements in an urban rehabilitation program. New apartment towers along East 55th Street near the Illinois Central tracks, plus townhouse mews along Harper, were some of the results of direct participation by the university.

Hyde Park–Kenwood became for purposes of federal financing an urban development zone. Federal funds were made available for street widening, park development, commercial centers, and public facilities. But unlike many a central city project, these urban features were planned to impart a new character to Hyde Park–Kenwood and at the same time retain a population, white and black, that could support the enclave economy needed to make Hyde Park–Kenwood work.

Hyde Park–Kenwood remains a residence for the university professor, the professional who wants to retain the aura of intellectuality and have the advantage of university presence nearby. It is also now the home of the upwardly mobile professional black who has made it and wants a quiet but quality residential neighborhood. Hyde Park–Kenwood is a success, however, largely because of the definitive role of the university. Unlike Columbia University in Morningside Heights, the University of Chicago chose not to become a landlord, though its holdings are not inconsiderable. Unlike Case Western Reserve in University Circle, the University of Chicago was able to preserve living space for the university community, whereas Case Western Reserve remains an unlived-in island surrounded by a sprawling ghetto on three sides.

The attempts to spread the positive effects of university-led neighborhood planning further south into the Woodlawn area from 61st Street to the 70s have largely been a failure. The decay immediately beyond stands in shocking contrast to the successes of Hyde Park–Kenwood even though some of the same potential elements of redevelopment are there. Is it that the university was unable to effect a renewal in an almost solidly black neighborhood? Is it that the drive to renew has simply run out beyond 61st Street? Or is it that enclave renewal requires the sense of enclave, if not the boundaries?

STANFORD UNIVERSITY IN THE SILICON VALLEY

Stanford University has always had a superb location. On the eastern side of the Coastal Range in Palo Alto, it sits between the Bayshore Freeway—US 101, the principal highway from San Francisco to San Jose—and I-280. Palo Alto is just over the line in Santa Clara County from San Mateo County, a county that has come to be known as Silicon Valley, the home of the semiconductor.

The corridor from San Francisco to San Jose is bounded on the east by San Francisco Bay, where the metropolitan regions of San Francisco, Oakland, and San Jose are located. This area has a concentration of almost 5 million people and is one of the key centers of finance, government, commerce, trade, industry, and manufacturing in the United States. In recent years the development of smokeless manufacturing facilities had led to high technology, electronics, and, especially, silicon chips. This industry requires a highly skilled labor force and a productive research and development capacity. The presence of laboratories and trained personnel as well as the faculty of a great university are essential to such industries.

The interaction between Stanford, the research facilities there and associated with it, and the industrial complex that has grown up along the Bayshore Freeway is a prime example of the way in which a university community can foster economic development.

The normal pattern of urban development in the United States has been to start with a transport node—a place where land transport lines (highways, railways, canals) meet—or a place where it was necessary to break bulk (a seaport, a lakeport, a riverport, or a terminal where penetration into a developable region tended to end (Denver, Salt Lake City, Bangor, Duluth-Superior). Around the activities of this transport node, commerce and industry grew up.

The interactive demands for land led to a pattern of city development. The typical pattern assigned to the central city (commerce, government, higher education, the church, social organizations) all forms of organized recreation and the control functions of society. Beyond the central city were industry, extensive transport land uses (railyards, grain elevators, docks, stockyards), and intermittent suburbs.

San Francisco and the Bay Area began this way. Only with the development of the auto and the freeway in the first twenty years of this century did this pattern change. The location of Stanford south of the city center along the Southern Pacific and within the rail-commuter zone made it possible to convert the area into a development node as the highway changed the interactive land-use pattern.

With the highway, the airport (along the Bayshore Freeway to the north of Palo Alto), and strikingly improved telecommunications, Stanford's position shifted from that with a purely suburban orientation to that of a center, a node for a highly specialized industry. That required what a world-class university had—research brainpower, management know-how, entrepreneurial talent, and the inclination to try anything at least once if only to learn something.

In a sense this was not so much a breakdown stage of intensive urban growth as an advanced highly specialized stage of industrial development. Having solved the basic problems of providing food, clothing, housing, mobility, and stability, the industrial complex of the United States turned to the tertiary problems of improving the quality of life, stepping up the pace of change, controlling the variations and vicissitudes of life, intensifying the effectiveness of communication of ideas—all of them changes making for a far greater integration of society. It is not surprising that universities were at the center of such developments.

What Silicon Valley provides is the basis for control. The "chip" permitted far better (faster) calculation and thus manipulation of data. It widened the area of calculability, turning the previously unmeasured or immeasurable into readily counted and controlled elements. The kind of mind needed to help develop and manage the technological advance was most likely to be found in a university setting.

The fact is, Silicon Valley attracted many firms and spawned many more. It was the fountainhead for creation of new jobs and the source of a massive increase in income that spread over almost all levels of society. To describe in a simple manner the interaction between Stanford and the San Mateo-Santa Clara community is difficult, though not impossible. One is tempted to try the very sort of model building that is now possible because of the level of technique developed in Silicon Valley.

THE UNIVERSITY AS AN INDUSTRIAL DEVELOPMENT CENTER

Research Triangle (Duke, North Carolina State, and University of North Carolina—Chapel Hill) and Ann Arbor (University of Michigan, Eastern Michigan University) are examples of induced development. In Research Triangle we have the planned effort of the university to assist in the development of Raleigh–Durham–Chapel Hill. Dating back to 1958, Research Triangle was located a short distance from three campuses and their facilities. The intention was to establish and coordinate scientific research in order to induce high-technology industrialization. The nonprofit Research Triangle Committee, Inc., was the vehicle for coordination.

Research Triangle Park was to be devoted to research and research-oriented manufacturing. The unique combination of business, government, and academic interests make for a complex structure and led some early observers to predict failure. In fact, however, Research Triangle has been an outstanding success. It has shown that organizations with dissimilar interests could work for a common developmental goal.

The measures of success that matter most are employment, investment, and change in the pace of growth of the region—even the state. Current levels of employment for activities directly related to Research Triangle exceed 10,000, with a payroll annually exceeding $200 million. Investments exceed a billion dollars, not counting indirect investments. But most important, this has become one of the centers of innovation in the nation and has given North Carolina a reputation for industrial leadership.

Though its purposes included retaining technical personnel, in fact that goal was the one most easily achieved and became overshadowed by another: it has become a lodestone for attracting scientific brainpower. Research conducted here includes work in textiles, chemistry, computer technology, forestry products, electronics, and medical science, to cite but a few. Research Triangle has spawned many firms that have subsequently gained national reputations.

The institutions and facilities at Research Triangle Park paint a vivid picture of the diversity and productivity of planned industrial research. What has developed is a community of the mind, a binding of creative talents to produce a center unique both in function and in substance. One of its founders, Luther H. Hodges, Sr., looking back at what has happened, said, "There is nothing quite like it anywhere else, in fact, in spirit or in purpose."[3] Exaggeration this may be, but Research Triangle has become a center to emulate.

In a state prone to considerable variation in employment over the business cycle and to substantial unemployment, the performance of the Raleigh-Durham labor market stands out. The average rate of growth of manufacturing jobs in the 1970s was 8.7 percent, significantly higher than the rest of the state. Overall growth in employment from the middle 1960s has increased more than 4 percent. In only two of these years has employment actually declined, 1967 and 1975, in sharp contrast with most other labor markets in the state and nation. These and similar data suggest that Research Triangle has made a difference not only in the pace of development but in the stability of that development of the Piedmont region of North Carolina.

ANN ARBOR AND THE UNIVERSITY OF MICHIGAN

Ann Arbor is a small city, prone to high unemployment. It is in a state that is also prone to high unemployment. More important, there is a wide fluctuation in the levels of employment accompanied by significantly varying levels of unemployment. This economic instability has become characteristic of the industrial Midwest. For labor-market areas like Ann Arbor, Flint, Bay City, Jackson, Saginaw, and Grand Rapids, and with the manufacturing share of employment exceeding 30 percent, that dependence has been both a blessing and a curse. Wages are high when men and women are at work, but periods of layoffs are frequent.

Over 20 million people live in cities and towns whose populations range from 25,000 to 100,000. The fact is that the economic problems of these places have been largely overlooked. The economies of many such cities and towns have contracted as key industries slowed down or left. Smaller cities find prosperity harder to achieve than larger cities, for definable economic reasons. Small cities lack large local markets and are often isolated from regional population centers. Often, they also lack high-quality transportation facilities. They sometimes have problems with shortages of skilled labor. Public services are of poorer quality than in larger, more metropolitan places.

Data show that small cities in the Northeast and the North Central regions have been growing at rates well below not only the national pace but their regions as well. In theory it ought to be easier to make economic adjustments in a place the size of Ann Arbor than elsewhere. But the facts are otherwise.

Local economies do not grow in isolation. The economy of a small city depends on its relationship with neighboring cities and major centers elsewhere. The effectiveness of an economic development policy or the effect of growth-poles as such can be analyzed from the magnitude of the policy or the growth-pole. The magnitude must be such as to offset the effect of broad market forces and the inherent disadvantages of being small. The emphasis may well be on activities that can be conducted anywhere, and here the university and its impact have the advantage.

The growth-pole concept, derived from the French economist, Francois Perroux, stresses the economic attractiveness of the key activity. The university is such a growth-pole. In this context a city does not need to be large or growing to provide an adequate economic base.

What is the role of the University of Michigan? Three things stand out. One is the development of high-technology plants along Plymouth Road from Ann Arbor into the nearby Detroit metro area. These owe much of their thrust to the spillover of technology and managerial talent from Ann Arbor. The second is the clustering of smokeless research type or consultative industry in Ann Arbor itself, as those associated with the university community have found ways to sell the know-how being developed there. Although the university is involved in both, its official role has been minimal while the role of the faculty has been significant.

The third factor is the increasing diversification of the economic base of the region to the west of Detroit. By the mid-1960s it was apparent that the automobile would not and could not provide the base for continued economic growth for Southeastern Michigan. It would continue to provide a limited number of high paying jobs with the accompanying employment instability characteristic of the industry, but a broadened manufacturing structure was necessary. Machine technology, chemical production, and electronics, among other industries, developed in the Ann Arbor labor market and eastward through Ypsilanti into the Detroit Standard Metropolitan Statistical Area along the Plymouth Road salient.

The employment growth rate for Ann Arbor's labor market averaged 5 percent in the 1960s, but fell to 1.8 percent in the 1970s. However, the more significant factor was the wide variation in employment growth rates in the 1970s. In 1976, for example, the number of jobs of all kinds grew an amazing 15 percent. In 1970 that growth rate fell almost 15 percent. It fell, too, in 1974 and 1975. It was this volatility that required a new job development strategy for Ann Arbor.

It was the spread effect of university growth and the spillover of university research and development in a wide variety of fields that made the latest recession less serious for Ann Arbor than for much of the rest of Michigan and the Middle West. The fact is that the new growth strategy is just under way, and it is also true that the university has not always sensed the precise role it should play.

BOULDER AND THE UNIVERSITY OF COLORADO

Up against the Front Range, Boulder isn't quite a Denver suburb, though it is linked with the metropolis by an expressway. Until recently it was possible to see along that expressway where the city's influence ended, and to mark off the separate existence of a college town that had always been an intellectual enclave. But that isolation is largely past as high-technology plants have filled in much of the empty industrial space along the corridor. The University of Colorado and the Colorado School of Mines in Golden, at the edge of the city of Denver, have a tradition of engineering and applied science. Not that there were not good liberal arts and sciences departments; it was just that if you thought of the typical Colorado graduate, he probably had a slide rule and more recently a calculator in his hands. It was a male world, oriented toward a frontier that wasn't quite tamed, despite the deceptive urbanity of Denver and the pleasant and easygoing ways of Boulder.

It is hard to say what changed that image. Part was surely finding new energy resources west and south of Denver. Part was the change in the nature of scientific application. It was no longer the engineer by himself but the scientist in his lab, and the products that could so easily be developed there. Part was the impetus to seek new industrial frontiers with the computer, automation, and sophisticated financial techniques. The university, itself a major landowner perforce in Boulder, played an active role in regional economic development.

The bringing together of university management, business leadership, and state industrial development types, along with aggressive bankers, created a much more explicit role for the University of Colorado than was the case in more aloof Palo Alto. But the effects were very much the same. The spillover from the university's know-how was massive and continuous.

It is not easy to spot where growth occurred first in the steady boom that Denver-Boulder has seen in the past ten years. Growth rates have a way of being aggregative and the state of the art of disaggregation in local statistics is by no means as well developed as the analyst would like. It would be wrong, however, to claim that growth moved out from Denver. The visual evidence is very much to the contrary. The thrust from the university and that from 17th Street melded somewhere nearer to Denver than to Boulder, according to university people. Whatever happened, we have another case of spillover. It is, moreover, another case of the university in regional development which results even without underlying explicit effort.

SUMMARY: INFERENCES AND POLICIES

Two things are evident from this research. One is that there is a variety of possible impact patterns resulting from the interaction of university and regional economic development. The other is that relatively little has been done to trace this interaction.

In these models we see essentially two kinds of development goals: one is to innovate by creating new industries and conditions; the other is to sustain, retain, and perhaps modify the region's economy. Clearly Research Triangle, Denver–Boulder–University of Colorado, and Palo Alto–Stanford are examples of the first set of goals at work. The second set applies to Ann Arbor and to Chicago. This we show in Table 1.

TABLE 1. Regional Developmental Goals

Regional Development Policies	Create/Innovate	Sustain/Retain/Modify
Direct		
Financing Investment Leadership Management	Research Triangle	University of Chicago (Hyde Park-Kenwood)
Indirect		
Support Consultation Atmosphere "Spillover"	University of Colorado (Boulder–Denver) Stanford University (Palo Alto–Silicon Valley)	Ann Arbor, University of Michigan

In Table 1, too, is a detailing of the basic differences in regional economic development policies. There are the direct policies of investment, financing, and providing leadership or management to the development effort. The examples of this set of policies are Research Triangle and the University of Chicago. Then there are the indirect policies, where the thrust is support, consultation, "spillover," and "atmosphere." These are exemplified in the cases of the University of Colorado, Stanford University, and the University of Michigan.

There is no clear evidence which of these policies is best, since "best" is largely a measurement *sui generis*. The ultimate question is the nature of the results obtained whatever the sources and the policy.

In Table 2 we summarize the evidence of the impact of economic development for each of the models of interaction. Also in Table 2 we rank the apparent impact by available measures of each university's interaction pattern. Thus we see that the impact of Research Triangle has been primarily in technological development, that of the University of Chicago in renewal of a decaying area, and that of the University of Michigan, economic stability in a volatile state. What emerges from these models is an overall ranking of impact.

Employment growth and changes in economic structure are the areas of greatest impact. Next in order is technological development. Then comes economic growth as such. Least important is renewal, with redirection of the economy as the next to the least important in this model set.

We have looked back over the past two or three decades at five examples of the university and its role in regional economic development. This is a setting for a forward look, at the potential for better interaction between the university and the region in New England. Clearly, one message emerges from this research. Whether or not a university or college has an explicit policy, there is such an interaction, a relationship that can readily be traced between what the university community does or does not do and the pace of regional economic development. Given the relative size of the university establishment not only in the region but in each of its subregions in New England, it could not be otherwise. Indeed, that interaction, as we have seen in Ann Arbor, Boulder-Denver, and Palo Alto can be highly effective even when there is no explicit university leadership.

Research Triangle indicates, however, what one or more universities can accomplish by explicit planning for perceived regional needs. The primary beneficiary may be the region, but there is no doubt that Duke, Chapel Hill, and North Carolina State have reaped a substantially higher national academic reputation. By contrast, when a university for survival reasons has tried to aid the renewal of the urban neighborhood where it is located, the interaction is in some ways simpler, in others more complex. The motivations may seem obvious but the traditional gap between town and gown is often a barrier to success. Thus the success of the University of Chicago is of more than passing interest, since

TABLE 2. Regional Economic Development Impact of University-Region Efforts

University Center	Employment Growth	Change in Economic Structure	Economic Growth	Economic Stability	Technology Development	Renewal	Redirection
Research Triangle	3	2	4	7	1	6	5
Stanford–Palo Alto	2	3	4	6	1	7	5
Chicago, Hyde Park–Kenwood	4	5	6	2	7	1	3
Colorado, Denver–Boulder	1	2	3	6	4	7	5
Ann Arbor, University of Michigan	4	2	3	1	5	7	6
Summary	14	14	20	22	18	28	24
Rank	1	1	3	4	2	6	5

what was accomplished was the enlisting of potentially opposing interests to save and advance an element of the urban economy.

To the evident question whether a college or university should want to help the economy of its region, the answer here seems to be that such help can hardly be avoided. It is not so much the help as the mutuality of the effort that is at issue. Who gets the benefit?

To the question what to do to advance regional economic development, there is no ready answer. One needs to scrutinize the goals of such proposed efforts. I cannot help concluding that there were in the above cases elements of both planning and happenstance. There were elements of benefit and cost. But in each, too, there was the almost inevitable widening of the horizon of the university community. The ultimate question is not whether but how to direct what will take place. And how to direct it to best mutual advantage.

5. INITIATIVES OF HIGHER EDUCATION TO ASSIST THE ECONOMY

Ward S. Curran

I propose in this chapter to show how higher education influences the New England economy now and how it could do so in the future. In the first part I use recent data on Gross Regional and Gross State Product for New England to describe the economies of the region and the states that comprise it. I rely heavily upon the research of others to indicate how the region arrived at its current economic mix.

Secondly, within the framework of the Gross State Product accounts I develop a series of data that indicate the work remaining to be done in order to develop a complete measure of the importance of higher education in gross state and gross regional product. I then turn to more conventional financial measures to discuss the importance of public and private higher education within the region.

In the third section I look briefly at the importance of high technology in the economic development of New England and the opportunities as well as the obstacles confronting higher education in exercising initiative in this area.

THE NEW ENGLAND ECONOMY TODAY

From Table 1 it is apparent that in 1978 New England accounted for 5.2 percent of the Gross Domestic Product of the United States,[1] with the bulk of the output concentrated in Connecticut and Massachusetts. Moreover, from Table 2 we can see that manufacturing, particularly durable goods manufacturing, is relatively more important in New England than in the United States as a whole.

Table 3 shows that within New England there are differences among the economies of various states. Manufacturing of nondurable goods is more important in Maine than is the production of durable goods. The opposite is true of the other five New England states. Finance, real estate, and the insurance industries play a greater role in the economies of Connecticut and to a lesser extent Massachusetts than these industries do in the other four states. Services, however, are more significant to

TABLE 1. Gross Domestic Product of New England and the United States (1978)

	GDP (billions)	GDP (% of national)	GDP (% of New England)
United States	$ 2107.0	100.0	
New England	109.4	5.2	100.0
Connecticut	31.8	1.5	29.1
Maine	7.4	0.4	6.8
Massachusetts	52.3	2.5	47.8
New Hampshire	6.8	0.3	6.2
Rhode Island	7.5	0.4	6.9
Vermont	3.6	0.2	3.3

Source: Grace On, "Gross State Product in the New England States," *New England Economic Indicators* (April, 1980); for detailed report see Grace On, *Gross State Product, New England,* Federal Reserve Bank of Boston, 1980. See also Lynn E. Browne, and John S. Strong, "New England–13th Largest Country," *New England Economic Indicators,* July 1980.

Massachusetts than to the other five New England states. Government plays a greater role in the economies of Maine and to a lesser extent Rhode Island than it does in the other four states. Finally, agriculture is more important in northern New England, particularly in Vermont and to a smaller degree Maine, than it is in southern New England. In none of these states does agriculture dominate the economy.

A deeper examination of the manufacturing component of the six states reveals how important a few groups of industries are (Table 4). Many of the capital goods industries classified under machinery, including and excluding electrical machinery, are important components of manufacturing of the economies of Connecticut, Massachusetts, New Hampshire, and, to a lesser extent, Vermont and Rhode Island. Fabrication of metal products as well as transportation equipment other than motor vehicles bulk large in Connecticut's economy. Miscellaneous manufacturing—which under Standard Industrial Classification (SIC)[2] includes jewelry, musical instruments, toys and sporting goods, office and art goods, brooms, brushes, and even burial caskets, account for the bulk of manufacturing in Rhode Island and Vermont. In Maine, however, paper, leather, food products, lumber, and wood are the major components of manufacturing. Textile mill products still play a role in the economies of Rhode Island and Vermont and to a lesser extent

TABLE 2. Relative Importance of Manufacturing in the Gross Domestic Product of the United States and New England, 1978
(percentage of current dollars)

	New England	United States
Manufacturing	28.7	24.1
Durable	19.3	14.4
Nondurable	9.4	9.7
Nonmanufacturing[a]	72.3	76.1
	100.0	100.0

[a]By industry, Nonmanufacturing would include wholesale and retail trade, finance, insurance and real estate, services, transportation, communications and public utilities, construction, government, mining and agriculture, forestry and fisheries.

Source: Calculated from data in Grace On, *Gross State Product, New England;* see also *Survey of Current Business* (April 1980), p. 14.

Maine, whereas instruments (including medical instruments, process-control instruments, etc.) are an important component of manufacturing in Massachusetts.

How the New England economy arrived at its current mix of output and services has been thoroughly discussed elsewhere.[3] At this point we shall confine ouselves to a presentation of the salient findings.

In the first place, although manufacturing remains relatively more important in New England than in the United States as a whole, some of that activity is being carried out with aging capital stock. At the same time, each state in the region, with the possible exception of Maine, is shifting with varying degrees of success into the high-technology durables.

Secondly, the comparatively poor endowment of natural resources (except for timber in Maine) ensures that the region will continue to be a major importer of food and raw materials, including fuel. To the extent that the prices of these items rise relative to the prices of other goods and services, the cost of living in New England will remain high relative to the nation as a whole.

A third finding counters the popular notion that New England is a high labor-cost region. Recent evidence suggests that hourly industrial earnings after allowance for regional differences in industrial structure and living costs are lower in New England than in other regions of the

TABLE 3. Relative Importance of Industries in the Gross Domestic Product of New England States, 1978 (percentage of current dollars)

	New England	Conn.	Maine	Mass.	N.H.	R.I.	Vermont
Manufacturing	28.7	30.9	28.1	26.6	30.9	32.4	27.5
Durable	19.3	23.4	10.4	17.5	19.3	22.4	20.6
Nondurable	9.4	7.5	17.7	9.1	11.6	10.0	6.9
Wholesale and retail trade	17.2	16.1	18.7	17.6	18.7	17.1	16.4
Finance, insurance and real estate	16.7	20.7	10.8	16.3	13.1	14.1	10.8
Services	15.5	13.5	13.5	17.4	13.7	14.7	15.2
Transportation, communications and public utilities	7.8	6.9	8.4	8.7	7.5	6.2	8.6
Construction	3.7	3.5	5.1	3.2	5.8	3.7	5.4
Government	9.5	7.6	12.9	9.8	9.3	11.4	9.9
Other[a]	0.9	0.8	2.5	0.4	1.0	0.4	6.2
	100.0	100.0	100.0	100.0	100.0	100.0	100.0

[a]This category consists of mining and agriculture.

Source: Calculated from data in Grace On, *Gross State Product, New England* (Boston: Federal Reserve Bank of Boston, 1980).

TABLE 4. Relative Importance of Specific Manufacturing Industries in New England (percentage of 1978 dollars)

	New England	Conn.	Maine	Mass.	N.H.	R.I.	Vermont
Manufacturing	100.0	100.0	100.0	100.0	100.0	100.0	100.0
Durable	67.3	75.8	37.0	65.6	62.6	69.0	67.7
Lumber and wood	2.2	0.5	15.0	0.9	4.9	0.4	0.4
Furniture and fixtures	1.0	0.8	0.7	0.9	1.3	0.7	0.7
Stone, clay, and glass	2.3	2.1	1.4	2.3	2.7	3.0	2.9
Primary metals	3.8	5.7	0.3	2.8	3.2	6.6	5.2
Fabricated metals	9.9	15.5	3.7	8.5	6.6	7.5	6.6
Machinery except electrical	14.5	15.5	3.7	15.5	20.8	8.8	8.1
Electrical	13.7	10.7	5.5	16.2	15.4	9.3	9.6
Motor vehicles	1.0	0.4	0.9	1.6	–	1.4	1.8
Transportation equipment except motor vehicles	8.0	16.8	4.6	4.5	0.5	3.3	3.0
Instruments	6.3	5.0	0.6	8.8	5.7	3.6	3.7
Miscellaneous manufacturing	4.6	2.8	0.6	3.6	1.5	24.4	25.7
Nondurable	32.7	24.2	63.0	34.4	37.4	31.0	32.3
Food and kindred products	4.5	3.2	9.7	4.9	3.8	3.3	3.5
Tobacco	0.2	0.5	–	–	–	–	–
Textile mill products	3.4	1.7	6.3	3.4	4.0	8.4	8.8
Apparel	2.4	1.4	2.3	3.4	1.6	1.9	2.3

TABLE 4. *(continued)*

	New England	Conn.	Maine	Mass.	N.H.	R.I.	Vermont
Paper	5.9	2.7	25.9	5.5	7.7	2.5	2.3
Printing and publishing	5.4	4.8	2.9	6.3	4.9	4.7	4.6
Chemicals	4.2	6.0	1.6	4.0	0.9	3.7	3.8
Petroleum refining	0.5	0.6	0.4	0.7	0.1	–	–
Rubber and miscellaneous plastics	4.1	3.1	3.1	4.3	8.7	5.2	5.5
Leather	2.1	0.2	10.8	1.9	5.7	1.3	1.5

Source: From data in Grace On, *Gross State Product, New England* (Boston: Federal Reserve Bank of Boston, 1980).

United States.[4] Moreover, along with the development of high-technology industries, it has been noted that such highly skilled professional services as medicine, management consulting, computer software, and higher education made up 13.2 percent of total employment in New England in 1978, compared with 9.7 percent of total employment for the United States as a whole.[5]

A fourth factor, one that needs further research, is the size of the pool of venture capital in this region and the likelihood that it will be directed toward the development of New England.[6] That this nation enjoys well-developed capital markets does not necessarily ensure that funds available in New England will necessarily be invested here. In seeking its highest opportunity cost commensurate with risk, capital may be more mobile than labor.

Finally, in terms of the personal income of its citizens the last several years have not been pleasant for New Englanders. The impact of the OPEC cartel on our energy supplies, the decline of older manufacturing industries like textiles and apparel, and the severe recession of 1974–75 all affected New England more severely than the United States as a whole.[7] As a result, relative growth in personal income has declined. From Table 5 we can see that from 1959 to 1964 the rate of growth in personal income for New England was slightly below that of the United States. From 1969 to 1978 the rate of growth was much less. Although per-capita personal income for the region remained one percent above the national average, a decline took place that was reflected with varying degrees of intensity in every New England state and in every Standard Metropolitan Statistical Area (SMSA). Moreover, the data are given in current dollars. Since living costs are greater for New England than for the nation as a whole, the relative drop in real terms would be somewhat larger. Having regressed toward the national average, whether New England will find itself in a few years below the average per capita income is a point to which we shall return later in the chapter.

EDUCATION IN NEW ENGLAND

An important element of the New England economy has long been the role played by private education. A recent report has suggested that private education is "more than twice as important an industry in New England as it is in the rest of the nation."[8] Although the statement is correct, there are differences among the New England states. To approach the problem from a perspective not generally used by others, and with the assistance of unpublished data from the Federal Reserve Bank of Boston, I have developed preliminary estimates of the relative importance of private educational services, including primary and secondary as well as higher education in 1978. In terms of personal income generated, the data from Table 6 indicate that although New England in 1978 accounted for 5.7 percent of the nation's personal income, it accounted for 14 percent of the personal income generated from private education.

From Table 7 we can see that as a percentage of Gross Private Domestic Product as well as a percentage of the service component of Gross Private Domestic Product, and with the exception of Maine, private education currently plays a greater role in the output of the economies of these states than it does for the nation as a whole.

Comparable data for public education—that is, as a percentage of the government component of Gross State Product—is not readily accessible. The same is true of data on private higher education as a component of private educational services. Should this approach to measuring the relative importance of higher education prove useful, further research will yield the necessary data. In the meantime, we shall fall back upon more conventional reporting procedures.

From Table 8 it is apparent that for the fiscal year 1977–78, the New England states accounted for 7.1 percent of the current fund expenditures of institutions of higher education, but only 3.5 percent of expenditures channeled through the public sector. On the other hand, New England accounted for 14.5 percent of the current fund expenditures that flow through the private sector.

That Massachusetts dominates the outcome is apparent in the data. Almost 80 percent of the current fund expenditures for higher education (Table 9) is in the private sector. There is no other state with a similar ratio. Indeed, outside of Connecticut, New Hampshire, and Rhode Island, only in Illinois, New York, and Pennsylvania do current fund expenditures for private institutions of higher education currently exceed those of public institutions.[9]

Among the New England states, the current fund reserves received from state and local governments as a percentage of personal income are below the national average; yet current fund expenditures as a percentage of personal income are above the national average—except in Connecticut and Maine (Table 10). Part of this anomaly can be explained by the relative importance of private education. When classified by control,

TABLE 5 Change in Personal and Per Capita Income for Selected Years for the United States and New England (current dollars)

	Average Annual Rate of Growth in Total Personal Income			Per Capita Personal Income					
				Dollars			% of U.S. Average		
	1959–69	1969–78	1959–78	1959	1969	1978	1959	1969	1978
United States	6.87	9.78	8.24	2,145	3,667	7,840	100	100	100
New England[a]	6.73	8.40	7.51	2,346	3,994	7,904	109	109	101
Connecticut	7.21	7.91	7.54	2,753	4,642	8,915	128	127	114
Bridgeport Stratford Norwalk Danbury	7.26	7.94	7.58	3,323	5,578	10,721	155	152	137
Hartford New Britain Bristol	7.38	7.88	7.61	2,667	4,486	8,671	124	122	111
New Haven Waterbury Meriden	6.56	7.61	7.06	2,565	4,262	8,163	120	116	104
New London Norwich	7.81	8.63	8.20	2,173	3,782	7,353	101	103	94
Maine	5.74	9.79	7.64	1,777	2,995	6,308	83	82	80
Portland	5.57	9.76	7.54	2,143	3,479	7,408	100	95	94
Massachusetts	6.47	8.16	7.27	2,359	3,999	7,926	110	109	101
Boston–Lowell Brockton-Lawrence Haverhill	6.53	8.17	7.30	2,465	4,173	8,306	115	114	106
New Bedford Fall River	6.46	8.73	7.53	2,015	3,381	6,715	94	92	86

TABLE 5 *(continued)*

	Average Annual Rate of Growth in Total Personal Income			Per Capita Personal Income					
				Dollars			% of U.S. Average		
	1959–69	1969–78	1959–78	1959	1969	1978	1959	1969	1978
Pittsfield	6.39	7.40	6.87	2,146	3,778	7,442	100	103	95
Springfield Chicopee Holyoke	6.09	7.83	6.91	2,217	3,660	7,117	103	100	91
Worcester Fitchburg Leominster	6.38	8.13	7.21	2,187	3,708	7,370	102	101	94
New Hampshire	7.46	10.77	9.02	2,091	3,535	7,378	97	96	94
Manchester Nashua	7.67	10.17	8.85	2,327	3,852	7,835	108	105	100
Rhode Island	6.36	8.30	7.28	2,138	3,643	7,447	100	99	95
Providence Warwick Pawtucket	6.35	8.49	7.36	2,145	3,663	7,514	100	100	96
Vermont	7.56	9.48	8.46	1,774	3,254	6,601	83	89	84
Burlington	9.10	9.58	9.33	1,911	3,501	6,865	89	95	88

[a]Figures for the average annual rate of change in total personal income and for personal income as a percentage of the U.S. average for New England were calculated from raw data.

Source: Survey of Current Business, Vol. 59, No. 8 Part II (August 1979), pp. 28–30, and Vol. 60, No. 4 (April 1980), pp. 25, 29–31, 35, 45, 52, 58, 63. State data for 1978 has been revised slightly in Vol. 60, No. 8 (August 1980), p. 58.

TABLE 6. Personal Income Total and Personal Income from Private Educational Services, for the United States and New England

(1978 dollars)

	Total Personal Income		Personal Income from Private Educational Services[a]	
	Millions of 1978 Dollars	% of Total	Millions of 1978 Dollars	% of Total
United States	1,709,616	100.0	12,005	100.0
New England	96,873	5.7	1,683	14.0
Connecticut	27,623	1.6	341	2.8
Maine	6,884	0.4	45	0.4
Massachusetts	45,765	2.7	1,061	8.8
New Hampshire	6,427	0.3	91	0.8
Rhode Island	6,960	0.4	100	0.8
Vermont	3,214	0.2	45	0.4

[a]Private educational services comprises elementary and secondary schools; colleges, universities, professional schools, and junior colleges; libraries and information centers; correspondence schools and vocational schools. See Executive Office of the President, Office of Management and Budget, Standard Industrial Classification Manual (Washington: U.S. Government Printing Office, 1972). Included in educational and general expenditures are mandatory transfers consisting largely of debt service. See American Institute of Certified Public Accountants, *Industry Audit Guide, Audits of Colleges and Universities.*

Source: Total personal income by state can be found in *Survey of Current Business* (April 1980), p. 25. Personal income from private education services was provided by courtesy of the Federal Reserve Bank of Boston.

TABLE 7. Private Educational Services as a Percentage of Gross Domestic Product and Service Industries for the United States and the New England States

(1978)

	% of Gross Domestic Product[a]	% of Service Component of Gross Domestic Product[a]
United States	0.7	5.3
New England	1.8	11.8
Connecticut	1.3	9.6
Maine	0.7	5.3
Massachusetts	2.4	13.8
New Hampshire	1.6	11.7
Rhode Island	1.6	10.8
Vermont	1.5	9.6

[a]For the United States the denominator employed in calculating the percentage is U.S. Gross Domestic Product or the service component of U.S. Gross Domestic Product. For New England the denominator is Gross Regional Product. For each state the denominator is Gross State Product for that state. The numerators in each case are personal income statistics for private higher education, made comparable with gross product using the procedure developed by John W. Kendrick and C. Milton Jaycox, "The Concept and Estimation of Gross State Product," *Southern Economic Journal,* 32, no. 2 (October 1965), pp. 153–168.

Source: Figures for U.S. Gross Domestic Product and the service component can be found in Lynn E. Browne and John S. Strong, "New England—13th Largest Country," *New England Economic Indicators* (July 1980), pp. A3, A4, and *Survey of Current Business* (May 1980), p. 14. Figures for Gross Product for the New England States and the service component can be found in Grace On, *Gross State Product, New England.* (Boston: Federal Reserve Bank of Boston, 1980). The personal income data for private educational services and gross product originating in this sector were provided courtesy of the Federal Reserve Bank of Boston. Private Educational Services comprise elementary and secondary schools; colleges, universities, professional schools, and junior colleges; libraries and information centers; and correspondence schools and vocational schools. See Executive Office of the President, Office of Management and Budget, Standard Industrial Classification (Washington: U.S. Government Printing Office, 1972).

current fund expenditures of public institutions of higher education as a percentage of personal income currently tend to be below the national average. Maine, New Hampshire, and Rhode Island are near the national average; Massachusetts and Connecticut are well below; and Vermont is well above. At the same time, current fund expenditures of private institutions of higher education as a percentage of personal income were higher than the national average for every New England state except Maine (Table 11).

TABLE 8. Current Fund Expenditures of Institutions[a] of Higher Education, by Control and by State, 1977–1978 (thousands of dollars)

	Total	% of U.S. Total	Public	% of U.S. Total	Private	% of U.S. Total
United States	45,970,790	100.0	30,725,119	66.8	15,245,671	33.2
New England	3,283,773	7.1	1,086,721	3.5	2,197,052	14.4
Connecticut	654,798	1.4	274,497	0.9	380,301	2.5
Maine	171,336	0.4	113,304	0.4	58,032	0.4
Massachusetts	1,840,830	4.0	387,477	1.3	1,453,353	9.5
New Hampshire	214,225	0.5	102,760	0.3	111,465	0.7
Rhode Island	249,905	0.5	118,983	0.4	130,922	0.9
Vermont	152,679	0.3	89,700	0.3	62,979	0.4

[a]Consists of all educational and general expenditures, including instruction, research, public service, libraries, maintenance, scholarships, auxiliary enterprises, hospitals, and independent operations.

Source: U.S. Department of Education, National Center for Education Statistics, *Digest of Education Statistics, 1980* (Washington: U.S. Government Printing Office), p. 155. Percentages have been calculated from raw data.

TABLE 9. Current Fund Expenditures[a] of Institutions of Higher Education, by Control and by State as a Percentage of Total Expenditures, 1977–1978

	% of Total Current Fund Expenditures by Control	
	Public	Private
United States	66.8	33.2
New England	33.1	66.1
Connecticut	41.9	58.1
Maine	66.1	33.9
Massachusetts	21.0	79.0
New Hampshire	48.0	52.0
Rhode Island	47.6	52.4
Vermont	58.8	41.2

[a]Consists of all educational and general expenditures, including instruction, research, public service libraries, maintenance, scholarships, auxiliary enterprises, hospital, and independent operations.

Source: Calculated from data in U.S. Department of Education, National Center for Education Statistics, *Digest of Education Statistics, 1980* (Washington: U.S. Government Printing Office), p. 155.

The relatively high figure for current fund expenditures as a percentage of income in Vermont is consistent with the fact that in 1978 at least it spent more per student for instruction in public higher education than any other state except Iowa. At the same time, state and local governments in Vermont appropriated less per full-time equivalent student than any of the forty-nine other states.[10]

New Hampshire relied more heavily on tuition and fees than any other state except Vermont. Similarly, except for Vermont, state and local government appropriations per full-time equivalent student are the lowest in the nation. New Hampshire, however, ranked 34th in terms of per-student expenditures for instruction. Rhode Island ranked 11th in tuition and fees, 9th in state and local appropriations, and 36th in per-student expenditures for instructions. Maine ranked 8th in reliance on tuition and fees and 47th in state and local appropriations. The state was tied with South Dakota at 41st in expenditures per student.[11]

At the opposite extreme, Massachusetts ranked 49th in its reliance on tuition and fees but 38th in appropriations of state and local governments. Per-student expenditures for instruction in public higher education in 1978 were lower in Massachusetts than in any other state. Meanwhile, Connecticut ranked 39th in reliance on tuition and fees but 27th

TABLE 10. Current Fund Expenditures and Current Fund Revenues Received from State and Local Governments for 1977–1978 as a Percentage of 1977 Personal Income

(United States and the New England states)

	Current Fund Expenditures[a] as % of Personal Income	Current Fund Revenues Received from State and Local Governments as % of Personal Income
United States	2.99	1.08
New England[b]	3.75	0.66
Connecticut	2.61	0.65
Maine	2.76	0.72
Massachusetts	4.42	0.61
New Hampshire	3.81	0.60
Rhode Island	3.96	1.02
Vermont	5.44	0.76

[a]Excludes U.S. Service Schools, which account for 0.9 percent of current fund expenditures.

[b]Calculated from the sum of current fund expenditures, current fund revenues from state and local governments, and personal income for the New England states.

Source: U.S. Department of Education, National Center for Education Statistics, *Digest of Education Statistics, 1980* (Washington: U.S. Government Printing Office, 1980), p. 156. Percentages were carried out to two decimal places in the source.

in state and local appropriations. That state ranked 46th in per-student expenditures for public institutions of higher education.[12]

There are important differences among the fiscal relationships between public higher education and state and local government. Although the data in Vermont and Massachusetts serve to illustrate the divergence in practices, it is clear that except for Vermont, per-student expenditures for instruction in public higher education in the New England states are currently among the sixteen lowest in the nation.[13]

THE ROLE OF HIGHER EDUCATION IN THE ECONOMIC DEVELOPMENT OF NEW ENGLAND

In sampling some of the returns of the questionnaire sent out by the New England Board of Higher Education to prominent leaders in education, state government, and business, I was struck by the belief on the part of many that the future of New England is intimately bound up with

TABLE 11. Current Fund Expenditures of Institutions of Higher Education for 1977–1978 by Control, as a Percentage of 1977 Personal Income (United States and the New England states)

	Current Fund Expenditures[a] as % of Personal Income	
	Public	Private
United States	2.0	1.0
New England States[b]	1.2	2.5
Connecticut	1.1	1.5
Maine	1.8	0.1
Massachusetts	0.9	3.4
New Hampshire	1.8	2.0
Rhode Island	1.9	2.1
Vermont	3.2	2.2

[a]Excludes U.S. Service Schools, which account for 0.9 percent of current fund expenditures.

[b]Calculated from the sum of current fund expenditures, and personal income for the New England States.

Source: U.S. Department of Education, National Center for Educational Statistics, *Digest of Education Statistics, 1980* (Washington: U.S. Government Printing Office, 1980), pp. 155, 156. Percentages calculated from raw data.

high-technology industries. Properly understood, there is substance to the opinion. As John Hekman has pointed out:

> If one looks at New England according to production process rather than final product, this region has shown remarkable constancy over the years. One of the major reasons for industry location in New England has been that the development of new products and production processes has taken place here.[14]

For example, the manufacture of firearms has been centered in Connecticut and central Massachusetts since Eli Whitney first produced rifles through the use of interchangeable parts. The machinery involved in this process helped to stimulate the machine-tool industry.[15] Some of these producers today are involved in the manufacture of computer-operated and numerically controlled products.

Technology, however, is the handmaiden of change. The mechanization of hand operations often hastens the outmigration of industry to areas closer to markets. As a result, the center of the machine-tool industry has moved to Cincinnati and Chicago. Gun manufacturing, however, remains in New England "because some facets of gun-making still require skilled operations, such as machining the rifle barrels."[16]

The decline or growth of textiles, computer-related equipment, jet engines, and medical instruments among others is related to technological development. New England is one of the few areas of the country that can offer both a broad range of high-technology suppliers and a skilled labor force. To the extent that this combination is necessary to achieve operational efficiency, industry prospers in New England. To the extent that automation of a process becomes the industry norm, relocation often results.[17]

High technology, of course, demands specific skills not only in assembling the products but also in continuing the process of development. A scientific and technical establishment is part of the pattern. These highly trained professionals can in turn form the nucleus for the research-oriented consulting firms, many of which are concentrated around the Boston area.

Consulting services also have a way of spreading into areas like economics and finance, which in turn may be useful not only to the manufacturing industries but also to insurance, banking, and other important sectors of the New England economy. Moreover, the output of these skills can be exported to other regions and nations.

The faculty employed in institutions of higher education can play a role both in the training of people to pursue these fields and as contributors in the research and development process. The former is part although certainly not all of the total education experience. The latter is often a function of individual initiative on the part of faculty.

A key question then is whether a more formal relationship among business, government, labor, and higher education will be useful in promoting economic development in New England. Sifting through the sample of the responses to the questionnaire distributed by the New England Board of Higher Education, the author found that in many but certainly not all cases there was little or no formal contact among leaders of these constituencies. Individual leaders do take initiative but there appears to be no consistent pattern of interaction.

Given a rather broad consensus that high technology and its occupational spin-offs including skilled professional services will be important to future growth in New England, the leaders of higher education would benefit from a more formal relationship with the other constituencies. These in turn must rely upon higher education for much of the research, analysis, and ideas necessary to promote economic development.

If a more formal relationship could prove fruitful, then why does the leadership of higher education not take the necessary initiative? There are, I submit, several reasons—all of them linked to institutional arrangements and tradition. They are difficult but not impossible to surmount.

In the first place, public institutions of higher education are more intimately related to the priorities of the state rather than the region. As our data on Gross State Product suggests, there are nuances in the relative importance of various industries in each of the New England states. High technology may have direct impact upon Boston, Hartford, New Haven, Providence, and the southern sections of Vermont, New Hampshire, and Maine, but its direct impact may not be felt in most of northern New England and in the rural areas of much of Massachusetts and Connecticut. Each state, therefore, is concerned first with its own pattern of development, and only secondly with its role within the region. Leadership of public institutions of higher education must first attune themselves to and perhaps even help shape the state's priorities. Although one cannot read a great deal from a single set of numbers, the relatively low per-student expenditures on public higher education in at least five of the New England states may attest to either a strong affinity for private education or the failure of government and ultimately the public to attach great importance to the industry.

For private higher education there are a different set of obstacles to overcome. Within the New England states lie at least three distinct groups—the national universities, the regional and urban universities, and the liberal arts colleges. Further subclassifications along religious and secular lines are feasible but for this discussion unnecessary. Of the three, the leadership and faculty of the regional universities, certainly those located in urban settings, are acutely aware that their survival may hinge upon continued growth and development of at least the regions from which they draw students.

Although some of the liberal arts colleges may also depend heavily upon New England for enrollments, others draw a large number of their students from the Middle Atlantic states and the Southeast. A few have students from all parts of the nation. Nevertheless, for all of them New England is an important source of students. Their ability to attract students is in large measure dependent upon the viability of the region. For liberal arts colleges perhaps a more troublesome issue concerns the curricular implications associated with the emphasis on high technology. The conventional wisdom is that although a substantive liberal arts education enhances one's analytical, verbal, and critical skills, it is not vocationally oriented. To be sure, a solid foundation in mathematics, English, etc. is important to the training necessary for learned professions, but that training follows not precedes an education in the liberal arts.

For the national universities, the major problem may be their willingness to give high priority to state and regional issues. They have contributed both directly and indirectly to the growth and development of local economies, but they have often paid scant attention to state and regional initiatives. Moreover, when located in urban centers, they have sometimes enjoyed an uneasy "town and gown" relationship.

None of these problems is insurmountable. In the face of declining numbers of 18 to 24-year-olds seeking entry into institutions of higher education in New England, it behooves its leaders to play a larger role in regional economic development.

We noted earlier in the paper that personal income in this region has regressed toward the average for the nation. We also pointed out that the recession of 1974–75 affected New England more severely than the nation. Moreover, in each of the post World War II recessions except one, the percentage drop in nonagricultural employment was greater in New England than in the rest of the nation.[18] Yet the shifts in the industrial mix that have taken place in the last several years may have helped to make New England somewhat less vulnerable to the national business cycle.[19] If so, there are grounds for optimism. High technology and professional service industries should play an important role in this renaissance. Higher education is a vital input in this process and is, therefore, a reason why government, business, and labor should seek to cooperate jointly with representatives of higher education to help plan for the future development of New England.

6. NEW ENGLAND'S RESILIENCE

Neal R. Peirce

In an age when the hot economic news is supposed to emanate from the Sunbelt, New England has pulled off something of a countercoup. The *Wall Street Journal*, *Time* magazine, the *New York Times*, the *Los Angeles Times* and other national journals have focused their attention in the past year on an unanticipated degree of prosperity and employment here. All of them talk of New England's now-fabled high-technology industries.

Indeed, it was the *Los Angeles Times*, from its publishing headquarters in distant California, which reported: "As the region that first faced the deep-seated, long-run ills that now plague much wider areas of the U.S. economy, New England has experienced a resurgence after decades of decline that provides an important perspective on the current political debate over what it will take to restore the U.S. economy to health."[1]

Yet in that inimitable style of America's best-defined region, the style that New England has refreshingly taken onto itself in field after field in recent years, leaders of the six states know they cannot afford to celebrate present success as much as to agonize over, and hopefully plan better for, the future. Indeed, for higher education the future promises a decline in enrollment of as much as 30 percent by the next decade, and the double threat that such a decline entails: a loss in the students and thus the dollars pouring into the region from outside that now undergird its economy, and a decline in college-educated persons at the very moment that manpower shortages are developing and promise to threaten that new jewel of New England's economy, high technology.

The less than salubrious outlook for college enrollments is not, of course, an exclusively New England phenomenon. The projections I have seen indicate that nationally, compared to a base year of 1979, high school graduating classes will be 18 percent smaller in 1986, 13 percent smaller in 1988, 26 percent smaller in 1991, and 22 percent smaller in 1995.[2] The problem is that for New England—and the states of Massachusetts, Connecticut, and Rhode Island in particular—the drop will be even more precipitous. The falloff there will be between 2 and 9 percentage points greater than the national dropoff in 1986, 17 to 23 points worse in 1991, and so on. Only in the Mid-Atlantic and North Central regions of the nation will the high school graduate decline be nearly as serious; conversely, in the Southeast and West, the dropoffs will be much smaller. Indeed, in 1995 Texas is expected to have 10 percent more high school graduates than in 1979, the same year the dropoff in the Northeast as a whole will be 38 percent.

Were I an educational planner in New England, I would see two major funding priorities for the future. First, I would ensure that school budgets decline at something comparable to the enrollment decline, for purposes of common-sense economy. Then I would transfer at least some of those savings into the area most chronically underfunded in New England, in comparison to the rest of the nation: public colleges and universities. And, of course, use those dollars to ensure that your public institutions make training for high-technology industries a major priority of the coming years.

The problems and opportunities go far deeper, however, than funding shifts. The root problem, as it has long been in New England, is to create and foster first the spirit, and then the fact of cooperative planning to deal with an ever-more complex and demanding regional condition. Some historical perspective should help to set the stage. When I wrote on New England, I was fascinated by the continual ups and downs—indeed, the periodic and fundamental changes—in the economy of this region over the centuries. Religious independence was apparently the first growth industry, the one that induced initial settlement. In agriculture the early settlers found a rocky landscape more exciting to the eye than susceptible to the plow. Yet resolutely and with a prodigious fortitude, they pressed into the primeval forests and onto the open lands once tilled by the Indians to create a strong agricultural base. First they farmed the most accessible lands along the coast and in the Connecticut River Valley. In 1796 one observer could write that the land between New Haven and Hartford was "a rich, well cultivated vale thickly settled and swarming with people." The thrust of farming went farther and farther north and higher and higher on the region's stony hills. Between 1830 and 1880 New England enjoyed the heyday of its self-sufficient farms and small villages. But then came the immense farming depression, as the Erie Canal and more particularly the advent of the railroads propelled New England farmers to forsake their ancestral homesteads and move into the broad and fertile fields of the Midwest.

It was a pattern to be repeated again and again. There was the growth of New England as a great maritime power, only to be eclipsed by New York and later Baltimore; the early rise here of insurance and banking, again to be overshadowed, at least in part, by Gotham; and of course the momentous New England industrial boom in textiles and shoes, only once again to lose out, after decades of prosperity, to the American Southland and then to less expensive foreign competition.

Yet on each occasion the region has staged a comeback phoenix-like—notwithstanding its location at the corner of the nation, its harsh climate, its lack of major natural resources. In my book I ventured a list of what made that possible: "A remarkable mix of pluck, luck, the China trade and clipper ships, technological innovation, cheap immigrant labor, tariffs, smart financing, wartime stimuli, and the momentum built by the region's headstart in the Industrial Revolution."

In the last few years, an even more interesting theory has been developed by Robert Eisenmenger and his colleagues, like Richard Syron of the Federal Reserve Bank of Boston. It is that New England, having been a fertile ground for innovative enterprises in its earliest years, has been able, again and again, to repeat the formula. According to this theory the textile industry was, in fact, New England's first high-technology industry. It had its genesis in 1790 in a daring act of industrial espionage by that young British immigrant, Samuel Slater, who brought to America, in his head, the secret design of the first power looms ever made. Slater's technology was then exploited by shrewd Yankee businessmen, largely out of capital generated by New England's seafaring successes, and by utilizing the power from the region's abundant and fast-flowing rivers. From the technology applied in textiles, machinery could be developed for the shoe, leather, paper, and, of course, machine-tool industries which followed.

In time, this theory goes, the new technologies become routinized and thus exportable. Boston College economist John Hekman, after a year of doing research at the Federal Reserve Bank in Boston, explained it this way: "Innovation occurs mainly in the established centers of the industry, especially when new products require high-technology resources and specialized goods and services. Mature, large-scale production, on the other hand, stresses mechanization and low-skill rather than high-skill labor. Mature industries look for locations that have low labor cost and ready access to markets." Hekman adds: "The key to beating the product cycle and industrial migration is not in keeping the industries at home, but in replacing them with new industries."[3]

Yet the residue of each wave of innovation is an invaluable base in finance, in skilled labor, in cheap but reusable old buildings, and, most critically, in the educational institutions that had been created with money donated by the magnates of the earlier industries.

This was precisely the pattern that permitted Ralph Flanders, the Vermont industrialist who headed the Federal Reserve Bank of Boston during World War II, to organize American Research and Development in 1946. American R & D started to finance aspiring young firms like Tracerlab and Digital Equipment. Many of these young firms were founded by Harvard and M.I.T. scientists, with the enterprises housed initially in abandoned old factories and warehouses. The rest of that story—to the rise of Route 128 as one of the world's foremost high-technology centers, to such firms as Data General, Wang Laboratories, Intermetrics, and so on, to the expansion along Route 495 and the Burlington high-technology base and little factories now expanding up to the northland—is well-known history, one marked at each step by the deep, ongoing interconnection between New England higher education and these high-growth industries.

Yet there remain severe problems with which New England must cope in this decade and beyond if it is to continue not just its favorable national press (a fickle asset at best), but truly broad and continuing economic development.

The declining enrollments in New England universities, coupled with the present and mounting manpower shortages in the high-technology area, are two of the greatest problems the region faces in the 1980s. Recently incredible figures were released on manpower needs, for instance: while Massachusetts' high-technology firms already employ 150,000 persons directly, they will require another 122,000 workers within a four-year period. Their job openings are increasing by about 22 percent a year.

To those problems we must add others, old and new: New England's continuing lack of natural resources, the dearth of fuels, high electric power costs, inherent locational disadvantages, adverse national tax policy, high construction and land prices, strict environmental laws (at least when applied in a blind bureaucratic way), as well as those factors on which James Howell of the First National Bank of Boston has so long dwelt: New England's traditional apathy and governmental fragmentation.

It is to the credit of farsighted New England leaders, dating back to the formation of the New England Council for Economic Development in the 1920s, that they have always insisted on New England's capacity to do for itself. They have never accepted the idea, so popular among economists, that the vertical, or top-down institutions of our society—the nation-state, national markets, national corporations, national unions, national media, and so on—render inconsequential the horizontal and integrating institutions of the region and state. Call it ornery Yankee independence, or self-reliant impulses born in Puritan days, or just common sense in defending one's own interests—New England leaders have always insisted that the region try to think and act for its own preservation and welfare. And it has done this despite the often discouraging climate for interregional cooperation that may have been born in the days of small and highly independent towns.

So the question arises: What can New England now do to improve and assure its future against the difficulties it faces? This chapter is not the occasion to address them all, but I will suggest approaches in some areas.

The common theme must be determination to mobilize as many of the institutions of the region as possible—regional organizations, state and local governments, universities, research institutions, and the illustrious high-technology firms themselves—in analyzing the region's chief problems and devising ways to attack those problems.

Let me start with the quandary of dropping university enrollments. I am most impressed by the opportunities in high-technology-related adult and career transition training which Ray Stata of Analog Devices, Inc., outlines below in Appendix II. I understand from figures assembled by John Hoy that only the top 10 percent of the 260 degree-granting universities and colleges of New England import students heavily from the rest of the country. Nevertheless, the net economic benefit for the region is reckoned in the millions.

One step might be for those universities to undertake a joint assessment of their areas of strength and weakness in research and education of students, and indeed in the intraregional sharing of educational facilities and resources, and then seek to correct the deficiencies which appear.

Following that, New England's colleges and universities might think of some intense joint promotion. As a parent of students already at or about to go to college, I have observed the phenomenal amount of promotional material that comes in by mail after they have registered their names with the Educational Testing Service. Why not then a cooperative New-England-wide promotion piece for students this region would like to recruit? I would think of a pamphlet—a thick one—that would highlight New England's position as an historically preeminent center of higher education, list the vast array of attractions here, from mountains and seashore to museums, galleries, theaters, and nightlife, and then contain a capsule paragraph on every college and university of the region. Each institution might star two or three of its strongest areas. Students across the country receiving such a pamphlet might indeed be impressed and drawn here if the preparation were highly professional and attractive. And one element could be to list the rich job opportunities that are indeed present and opening up to college graduates in these six states.

Concurrently there could be a national promotion campaign to draw fresh college graduates, and in fact talented people up to middle age, into New England to fill the jobs that are now going begging. There ought to be plenty of room: in southern New England especially, population figures are static or close to it, with strong outmigration. Indeed, with the immense labor shortages developing within the high-technology firms, it need not be left to those companies individually to try to recruit into the region the engineers and others needed to fill their job openings. A strong public commitment to worker recruitment into the region would, in fact, encourage these firms to keep and expand more of their facilities here.

How might such a cooperative recruitment effort be undertaken? A few ideas spring immediately to mind. Advertisements, especially in specialized journals and magazines, could play a part. So might recruitment teams dispatched to campuses around the country, jointly representing a broad range of New England firms. One might simply reprint and distribute some of those glowing newspaper accounts, from the *Wall Street Journal* or the *Los Angeles Times*, about the robust condition and opportunities here. This is a job that major New England advertising firms could do well. And, to the degree that journalistic integrity would permit it, so might newspapers and New England-based magazines.

In such promotional efforts, one could think especially of the problems that young people face in finding affordable housing. Buying the first house or space in a condominium—a way to get a toehold on the ever-inflating housing escalator—is an immense problem for the members of today's baby boom generation. What if high-technology firms, insurance firms, banks, and state and city governments, perhaps even universities, cooperated in constructing such housing in locations convenient to the worker-short firms? Proximity to employment, as well as urban amenities, are strong drawing cards today—factors to be kept in mind as one attempts, in matter of fact, to manage housing demand in relation to employment.

As in advertising for college students, strong emphasis might also be placed on New England's impressive array of cultural and natural amenities. I would be so bold as to suggest that the strong environmental laws now in place in several New England states could be an attraction. For young people today, clean air and water, curbs on tasteless sprawl, and park and recreation opportunities are very important. Frequently business leaders say that environmental laws discourage industry. Perhaps they do in some cases, but the reverse side of the coin is that a clean, neat, treasured natural environment, along with healthy and compact towns and cities, are strong drawing cards. The areas with which New England competes—Texas, California's Silicon Valley in Santa Clara County, and so on—enjoy milder weather, but they are now facing ever-more-severe environmental problems caused by their own callousness and lack of planning. New England has strong advantages here; it must exploit them to the hilt to overcome its drawbacks: long winters, slushy springs, high home-heating costs, and high taxes.

Next I think one needs to recognize that not every job opportunity lies in the high-technology area. There are differences in manpower needs among the firms themselves. Moreover, their spinoff require immense varieties of ancillary services. And there are other promising areas of the economy awaiting exploitation. My observation is that few state or local governments do anything approaching an adequate job of predicting future manpower needs.

The same applies to the universities, which ought to be in the business of training those future work forces. Yet the federal Department of Labor does detailed manpower demand projections, down to a county level. And the skills surely exist in New England universities and research institutions to take the Labor Department figures and refine them for regional need, or indeed to develop projections on their own.

Manpower-need forecasts are vital not just in the high-technology field, but also for the bulk of New England colleges educating native

New Englanders for jobs in a broad array of fields. There have been complaints that this region's institutions of higher learning don't train for real life jobs. That's a clear shortcoming and, of course, needs correction, although I would add here, parenthetically, a plea not to forget the values of a broad liberal education. At a regional seminar of the Education Commission of the States, held in Boothbay Harbor in 1979, a telling remark was made by Dorothy Goodwin, house chairman of the Connecticut Legislature's education committee. Reacting to pleas to fashion curricula for job purposes alone, she said: "You people frighten me when you start talking about people as if they were widgets." The emphasis on the training aspect of education, she noted, can overlook the longer-range reality for the individual, which is the "job beyond the first job" to which the broader responsibility of higher education should be directed. The point is well taken. Not that one fails to undertake manpower-needs analysis, but that one retains the base for offering a liberal education, even one for engineers. We need a populace educated in the broadest sense of the word, with universities turning out graduates capable of being citizens and leaders as well as technicians. New England, birthplace of higher education on this continent, ought instinctively to recognize that need—as, indeed, such great scientific institutions as M.I.T. have in recent years, with their broadening humanities curriculum.

Is New England, with its strong emphasis on prestigious, high-grade education, also looking into the full variety of R & D spinoffs that could well occur in this region? In energy firms, financial services, gene-splitting, assorted medical areas? Perhaps so. But this region cannot afford to rest on its laurels. It is New England research, conducted by David Birch at M.I.T., that is now demonstrating to the nation the immense growth potential in small and medium-sized firms as opposed to the famous ones on the *Fortune* lists of the 500 and 1000 largest industrials. The biggest firms, in fact, have been experiencing negligible net nationwide employment gains. It is the growth rate of small firms, and expansion rates of small and medium-sized ones, that are truly determinate of an area's economic health. This is because the death rate of firms seems fairly constant across the nation, and actual moves of major industries from one part of the nation to another are fairly rare occurrences. If small is beautiful and birth the vital factor in economic planning and growth, what is New England doing to encourage the creation of new firms? Are there state or local efforts to encourage new entrepreneurs—to help them in planning, budgeting, management, marketing, and locating capital? I know of some such efforts in New England—yet I seriously doubt if there are enough.

It goes without saying that all such efforts should be coordinated with university research, the spawning ground of so much growth here in recent years. I might add that while the most exciting breakthroughs may come in sophisticated and high-technology areas, the universities—through their departments of economics and urban affairs—can also help mightily with those left-out people of the region. In helping, for instance, neighborhood groups become contractors for the delivery of social services, and then move on to the creation of their own community-development corporations and other economic enterprises to create a base of economic self-sufficiency in long down-and-out areas.

The universities also bear a major responsibility, I believe, in the area of elementary and secondary education. Across the country, one hears a chorus of complaint from colleges about the poor quality of students they are receiving today—students unable to read, write, comprehend, or conceptualize adequately. Yet is it too indelicate to ask who trained the teachers who failed to instill those basic skills in young people as they passed through the schools? You know the answer—those very same institutions of higher learning, now ensnared in their own nets of pedagogical training without emphasis on content, in tenure and over-credentialing, and all the abuses so abundantly reported in recent years.

The time is overripe in this country to introduce a healthy measure of political accountability into publicly supported education. Ellis Katz of the Temple University Center for the Study of Federalism has noted:

> For generations, the educational community struggled to remove education from the political arena. Behind a posture of professional expertise, it succeeded in having school board elections separated from general elections, giving local school districts independent taxing power, granting tenure to system professionals and settling policy disputes among themselves.[4]

But today, Katz notes, "public dissatisfaction with the schools, the rapidly growing cost of education, and the development of special interest groups have combined to thrust education squarely into the political arena."

That really is, I believe, to the good. Americans are increasingly impatient with unaccountable professional cadres. If war is too important to be left to the generals, then education is too important to be left to the professional educators.

State legislatures, their well-advertised shortcomings notwithstanding, should be looked to for leadership in this area. As New York State Assemblyman Leonard Stavisky has observed: "State legislatures are in a unique position to receive and reconcile the views of the different groups interested in education. As catalysts and conciliators, as advocates and arbitrators, individual lawmakers and legislative institutions can provide leadership by insisting on statewide standards, exercising programmatic and fiscal oversight, and evaluating the performance of all players in the educational area."[5]

Personally I believe that principle should be followed through by making public colleges and universities, as well as school districts, more responsible to, and thus more responsive to, general-purpose elected government. Our states and communities will face some very tough choices in this decade and beyond. They must be able to mobilize all their resources to cope with deep problems in such areas as employment and energy. But they can't do that if education is left in some hermetically sealed outside department. Does that mean throwing public education into politics? Yes, it does. The problem is to show Americans, by examples of excellence, that politics is an honorable profession, indeed the people's own forum, and linked to the very issues of regional survival and growth discussed in this book. Hiding behind professional barriers is a cop-out.

Yet the science of instruction itself should not be ignored. A number of studies indicate that the quality of a school principal is the most important variable in a school's overall quality and student performance. Such areas require careful study of the screening, training, and evaluation of principals, if indeed they make such a crucial difference. And, it is in our university-level departments of education that such research should begin.

The universities that train our teachers also bear a special responsibility in a field of great importance to the society: civics and history teaching. If indeed it is one's goal not just to train a qualified labor force for the region, but also to create bonds of identity and loyalty to keep that labor force here over the years, then the schools present a golden opportunity. Of all regions of America, New England has one of the most fascinating histories and traditions—and so do its individual states. One might seriously consider for high schools a mandatory year's instruction in state and regional history, provided of course that a stimulating and high quality text were available, presumably written within New England universities. Such instruction and text are not irrelevant to a region's long-term economic future: to the contrary they are part and parcel of it. Both public and private institutions of higher learning should be encouraged to include more in their curriculum, and their areas of research concern, on New England—its history, economy, and literary traditions.

Where are the great regional scholars in New England universities today? One finds very few. Not enough new John Perry Millers. The burden of regional economic research, for instance, has passed from Cambridge to such institutions as the Federal Reserve Bank and the First National Bank of Boston. Apparently regional studies don't give an academic great points in his or her search for tenure and peer recognition. The same all too often applies to urban studies in the politics field. Well, if this is so, especially in public institutions, then I believe the legislatures have a right and responsibility to insist on change.

In closing this chapter, I would like to focus on the issue of corporate funding of higher education.

According to figures from the Council for Financial Aid to Education, corporate gifts to colleges and universities accounted for less than one percent of their total income in 1978–79. This has not always been so: before World War II, industry supplied a substantial share of university research budgets. But after the war the federal government got into the university research field and in fact took it over. The net result, observes an official of Air Products and Chemicals Inc., is that "the professors are working on what's important for Washington rather than what industry needs." And yet we can look across the seas to Japan and note that one reason for that nation's phenomenal industrial rise is the close university-business collaboration that exists there.

There are problems in direct industrial funding of university research. They range from abstract notions of academic freedom and the profit motive to pragmatic considerations of patents, trade secrets, and publication privileges. J. W. Peltason, president of the American Council on Education, is right on target when he says: "In higher education, we talk to ourselves too much. So do business leaders. It is time for leaders of education to sit down and talk to leaders of business." The survey results reported in Melvin Bernstein's introductory chapter seem to undergird that conclusion.

And to this observation one can add the thought: Where more so than in New England, with its world-renowned educational institutions, its advanced industries, and their immense joint potential to plan and build the future? I should think there would be great opportunities in direct research grants to New England universities from New England firms. And also, for scholarship programs sponsored by New England firms for students choosing New England colleges and perhaps making an informal commitment to begin their professional lives here later on.

Indeed, whether the issue be corporate giving, promotion of New England as a place to learn or work, the quality of the schools and public universities, or any of the other areas I have covered in this chapter, the themes are remarkably parallel. They add up to a compelling necessity for New England, America's first defined geographic region, the cradle of a nation's civilization, to gird itself for a struggle to maintain its economic strength, its reservoir of talented persons and great institutions, and in that struggle to use the immense resources, built and nurtured over centuries of development, that are now available to it. I believe New England owes itself and its people no less.

7. EXPANDING HIGHER EDUCATION'S ROLE IN NEW ENGLAND'S ECONOMIC DEVELOPMENT

Robert E. McGarrah

My purpose is to address two questions: Why should institutions of higher education want to help the economy of the region? How can these institutions help? My discussion will focus on New England, although it is applicable to all regions. New Englanders have lived longest with problems of the postindustrial era, and with fewer industrial, agricultural, or energy resources. Their colleges and universities are numerous and well-established, and my experiences with the university's role as honest broker or activating catalyst for regional economic development have been mainly in New England.

WHY SHOULD THEY HELP?

Colleges and universities should want to help the economy of their communities or regions of interest for at least five reasons, all interrelated.

HIGHER EDUCATION HAS CONSTITUTIONAL OBLIGATIONS

Since the Morrill Act of 1862, Americans have given more of their wealth, intellectual talents, and youth to higher education than has any other nation in history. We have looked to the university not just as a certifier of necessary credentials for future leaders, but also, and more important, as a wellspring for the moral and intellectual enlightenment all Americans need to preserve our constitutional liberties and to practice democratic self-governance. We want as many citizens as possible to participate in governing affairs of all institutions or professions. Whether they are financed from public or private sources, our colleges and universities are chartered to serve our pluralistic, diverse, yet common intellectual needs to maintain "a more perfect union, to establish justice, insure domestic tranquility, provide for a common defense, promote the general welfare, and secure the blessings of liberty to ourselves and our posterity."

Since Vietnam and Watergate, the American social fabric of traditional optimism and faith in progress has been under increasing strain from apparent failures—to reduce inflation and unemployment, to stop the American decline in productivity or loss of shares of the U.S. and global markets for automobiles, steel, electronic equipment; to develop a consensus and common commitment on the conservation, development, and uses of energy; or to quell the growth of apathy, resignation, cynicism, or fears of militant special-interest groups who demonstrate few concerns for the commonwealth. Perhaps all Americans—rich and poor, black and white, young and old—are discouraged because gaps between promise and performance of our industry and government seem to grow wider. Yet Americans continue to trust our colleges and universities as a source of enlightenment.

At age 18 American youth is enfranchised to vote, required to register for military service, and offered opportunities for higher education. Along with obligations for seeking truth and upholding standards of academic excellence, it can be argued that our colleges and universities have a constitutional obligation to educate students in the responsibilities of industry, government, and the professions in order to manage processes for cultural and economic development more effectively.

HIGHER EDUCATION SERVES NEEDS FOR CULTURAL WITH ECONOMIC DEVELOPMENT

Among all institutions involved in economic development, colleges and universities stand unique. They possess and use the widest range of intellectual and professional capabilities for cultural development *with* economic development.

The history of New England, Appalachia, and other regions indicates that if cultural development is ignored, taken for granted, or otherwise subsumed by processes for economic development, the social or environmental consequences could be difficult, perhaps even intolerable.

The Morrill Act gave to state universities the role of serving as catalyst to the establishment of what we know today as the agribusiness-government complex. Although this complex developed ever higher capital-and-energy-intensive methods to increase production of foods and fibers, it has also been a cause of the migration of poor, unskilled people from family farms. Today less than 5 percent of our population produces all food for American needs, not only for consumption but for exports to foreign markets. This amazing growth in productivity and influence on American agriculture has been a model for economic development of many societies. But cultural disruptions have been severe, here and abroad. Our cities still struggle with concentrated burdens of poverty, rising crime, unemployment, decaying property values, and risks of financial bankruptcy. And there are increasing concerns that methods of the agribusiness-government complex have caused serious erosion of topsoil essential to sustain productive growth of foods and fibers. If the university as a whole had paid more attention to cultural and ecological efforts of agricultural specialists, perhaps cultural problems might be less acute.

Compared with other regions of the United States, New England possesses few energy, material, or land resources for capital-intensive manufacturing or agricultural industries. Perhaps like Switzerland or Japan, New England's human talents and its Puritan work ethic are its strongest resources for economic growth. Historically, the people of New England pioneered in the production and uses of hydropower, coal, petroleum, nuclear energy, and renewable energy sources. But risks of environmental pollution and dangers to health and safety are approaching our limits of toleration. And costs of imported energy are already highest in the United States. It is clear that further economic development in New England requires growth of more labor-intensive, less energy-intensive kinds of enterprise.

HIGHER EDUCATION IS ALREADY A MAJOR ENTERPRISE FOR ECONOMIC DEVELOPMENT

A major challenge is to select the kinds of enterprise through which maximum numbers of New Englanders can and would work for more effective development of their region. In this light New England higher education has already proved to be a significant enterprise, perhaps more so than generally realized.

There are 260 universities, four-year colleges, and other postsecondary institutions scattered among rural communities and cities throughout the region.[1] Boston has been described as "not just a college town, but America's college city."[2] Amherst College, Hampshire College, Smith College, Mt. Holyoke College, and the University of Massachusetts exert strong influences on the culture, commerce, and employment of citizens of the Connecticut River Valley.

During the fall of 1979 there were 738,000 students enrolled in institutions of New England higher education. Of 400,982 enrolled in Massachusetts colleges during the fall of 1979, about 100,000 were

Americans from other states, and 3,210 were citizens from foreign nations.[3] The Massachusetts Taxpayers' Association estimated that about 11 percent of Americans attending colleges or universities outside their home state are enrolled in Massachusetts institutions.[4] With U.S. average student costs in 1979–80 of about $3,376 at public institutions and $5,733 at private institutions, revenues brought into New England by higher education have ranged, conservatively, between $170 and $180 million each year. I say conservatively because in making this estimate I did not impute income from endowments, grants, or gifts or from visitors (parents, academicians, friends, etc.) to New England colleges and universities from sources outside the region.

Employment, budgeted expenditures, and endowments for higher education in New England are also significant. Employment and enrollment statistics indicated that about 7.5 percent of the New England population was involved in higher education. Budgeted expenditures totaled about $3.2 billion during the academic year 1978–79.[5] Of the top 75 U.S. colleges and universities ranked according to the market value of investments as of June 30, 1979, New England institutions were most numerous: 17 with a total endowment of about $3.5 billion, or 32 percent of the $11.3 billion for the 75 institutions.[6]

New England higher education is acknowledged throughout the world to be of the highest quality in every field: fine arts, performing arts, humanities, physical and life sciences, engineering, law, public health and medicine, business, and public administration. Consequently, higher education has made New England a center for concentration of many diverse and fast-growing institutions closely dependent on its colleges and universities. For examples: high-technology, computer-electronic-defense systems development; think-tank research and consulting firms in fields of physics; biological and chemical and health sciences; political science and international relations. The Massachusetts Council on the Arts and Humanities found that musical concerts, lectures, and art exhibits, most of which are held at colleges and universities, add $320 million to that state's economy, and employ 14,000 people.[7] Colleges and universities are focal points for frequent conferences or conventions of intellectuals or professionals, along with intercollegiate sports events. Thus they provide a major contribution to the growth of New England industries for hotel, restaurant, travel, and recreation.

Colleges and universities have shown a remarkable stability about their growth in enrollment. During the Great Depression of the 1930s and subsequent periods of rising unemployment, their enrollment continued to rise, steadily. Convictions remain strong that higher education gives assurances of better economic and cultural opportunities. Despite more stringent limits to the growth of the U.S. student population, enrollment at New England colleges and universities has continued to increase faster than enrollment at other U.S. institutions.[8] This is another indication of the importance of the high-quality education offered by New England colleges and universities.

They are well-positioned to encourage broadly based, steady economic development with fewer political or demographic disruptions than are likely to occur with growth of other kinds of industries. Consider high technology, for example. Although acknowledged to be a most promising contributor to New England economic development, the rapid growth of high-technology manufacturing means that in the greater Boston area there is likely to be a large concentration of employed physical scientists and engineers. They will represent a narrow range of diverse talents and needs of New Englanders. Too much emphasis on the growth of high-technology industry could create difficult problems of socioeconomic cohesion. Gaps would grow wider between citizens who do and citizens who do not belong to that specialized industry. Moreover, high-technology products may become vulnerable to cyclical market fluctuations of defense industries, or to the sort of fierce competition from Japanese and European firms in the U.S. and global markets experienced in recent years by American automobile and steel manufacturers.

New England colleges and universities have already enhanced a broadly based economic growth. They are labor-intensive and provide steady employment for people with all kinds and levels of talents. They are held in high esteem and are strongly supported by people of all races or socioeconomic classes. They do not cause hazards to health or the natural environment, and their energy consumption is geared to human needs. They are leaders in efforts both to conserve and to expand sources and uses of energy needed for further development of any region, not just New England. They attract large investments and revenues from outside the region, not just by their own operations as centers of academic excellence, but by spawning and stimulating new enterprises for growth of agricultural, manufacturing, and service industries.

ECONOMIC DEVELOPMENT MEANS MORE DEPENDENCE ON KNOWLEDGE

It is evident that in our postindustrial era of "reindustrialization," economic development processes will become more complex and therefore much more dependent on *knowledge*, which is the business of higher education. Government, industry, or the professions can conduct more complex processes for economic development only if colleges and universities provide more intellectual talents needed to manage those processes for the common good. The development and applications of science and technology mean that knowledge per se is power. The college and university can no longer concern itself solely with traditional academic freedom to pursue knowledge for its own sake. Society is demanding and colleges and universities must provide more and better education in uses and abuses of knowledge and powers of industry and government, for important reasons: rising unemployment; poverty and crime; increasing hazards to human and environmental health; increasing risks of nuclear accidents, terrorism, or war. Higher education must participate in the cultural and economic development of more peaceful interdependence among communities, regions, and nations.

Government and industry have a long tradition of institutionalized dependence on higher education. They have sponsored academically accredited higher-educational institutions. Examples: the academies for the U.S. Army, Navy, and Air Force; General Motors Institute; executive development programs at Harvard, MIT, Stanford, Columbia. As noted earlier, there have been complexes of governmental, industrial, and university cooperation for specialized research and development in fields of agriculture, health, and armaments. Moreover, although acting more as individuals than as agents of higher education, faculty members in the sciences, engineering, and management have performed extensive research, consultation, and continuing education services for industry and government.

Although these services created wealth and influential positions for many faculty entrepreneurs, the university, *as an institution*, has benefited only indirectly, if at all. Indeed, since the 1960s there have been strong protests against the university's complicity with special-interest bureaucracies of government and industry on grounds that those *special* interests conflict with *universal* interests of higher education. So universities divested themselves from such organizations as Stanford Research

Institute, Cornell Aeronautical Laboratories, and the Institute for Defense Analysis.

But as already suggested, higher education cannot remain aloof from processes for economic development which demand better qualities of intellectualism. So the question is how purposes of higher education can be sustained while colleges and universities expand their role in regional economic development. I do not believe that leaders of higher education can decide whether or not, but only *how* to expand their college or university's role, because bonds of society's dependence on higher education *and* economic development are too strong. Also, there is mounting evidence that for financial reasons higher educational institutions will have to take their own initiatives in economic development affairs.

HIGHER EDUCATION NEEDS MORE FUNDS THAN PHILANTHROPY IS LIKELY TO PROVIDE

Colleges and universities have depended traditionally and very substantially on philanthropic sources of funds: grants, gifts, endowments, subsidized loans, or appropriations of public and private funds. Tuition revenues, which have sustained only about one half of operating expenditures, cannot be increased without risk of exacerbating effects of a decline in the pool of high school graduates—a decline estimated at 35 percent by 1991.[9] And because of inflation, health, welfare, poverty, and many other problems that demand funding of higher priority, it seems apparent that philanthropic sources of funds for higher education will not grow as rapidly as needs of funds for more basic research or improved curricula.

Thus in addition to their efforts to solicit grants or gifts or to lobby for higher appropriations of public funds, colleges and universities are likely to exploit their capabilities for *earning* revenues they need. In other words, they will generate their own income by acting as another enterprise in markets of the "knowledge industry," providing research and educational services needed for economic development in the 1980s.

To sum up, colleges and universities should want to expand their role in regional economic development because they have a constitutional obligation to do so; because they have unique capabilities for cultural development, without which economic development, alone, would be meaningless; because they are already New England's wellspring-enterprise for developing its "knowledge industries"; because future economic development of New England requires more knowledge and skills; and because higher educational institutions can no longer depend solely on philanthropic sources of funds, but must act more as an enterprise to generate funds needed for cultural and economic development of New England.

HOW CAN THEY HELP?

MORE COOPERATION AND LESS COMPETITION BETWEEN PUBLIC AND PRIVATE HIGHER EDUCATION

There has been a long-smoldering conflict between public and private higher education. If continued, it will seriously jeopardize possibilities for expanding the role of higher education in regional economic development.

The conflict between advocates of the two sectors tends to violate their responsibility to provide for people's intellectual needs. With its more numerous, long-established, private institutions and its fast-growing, younger, state institutions this conflict is, perhaps, more intense in New England. And with prospects of more severe limits to growth of funds, enrollment, faculty, and curricula of both private and public institutions, competition may become more intense.

Protagonists of public institutions allege that private institutions do not serve needs of intellectually capable students of the low socioeconomic classes; that they use their stronger established powers unfairly to gain concessions from government by way of grants or subsidized loans for new facilities, research projects, or financial aid for students; that private colleges encourage upper-class elitism, repress socioeconomic mobility, and thus reinforce rigidities of social strata like those of British society; that the very existence of such a large number (167) of private New England institutions has prevented the growth of institutions for public higher education in New England. The influence of private colleges and universities explains why Massachusetts' funding support for public higher education ranks number 49 of the 50 states.

Protagonists of private higher education allege that standards of intellectual quality at public colleges are low because these institutions must admit graduates of any and all secondary schools, regardless of their intellectual capabilities; that curricula at public colleges lack academic substance or rigor because they are too vocational or too repetitive of curricula at high schools or preparatory schools; that public colleges cannot freely select students, faculty, or curricula because they are chartered to serve public interests, not academic interests; that more public funds should be channeled to private institutions precisely because they are most capable to preserve qualities of intellectual excellence essential to national or social security, and because sources of private funds are becoming more scarce.

The conflict over the proper roles and relations of public and private interests in higher education continues, only occasionally by way of ongoing public debate; more often there have been charges and countercharges of conspiratorial maneuvers or lobbying behind the scenes. Antagonisms are likely to grow more bitter as problems of declining enrollments and income become more serious. If leaders of public and private higher education should fail to transform their competition into cooperation, they could destroy the very qualities that gave New England colleges and universities a strong basis for cultural and economic development.

Why should the intellectual content of curricula and programs be different in private colleges from those in public colleges? The pursuit of truth and of better ways to apply knowledge to serve mankind are common purposes of all higher education. Associations of scholars do not distinguish the status of their members because of their affiliations with public or private universities. Although novelists, playwrights, or pundits have created or resonated impressions that the "establishment" of prestigious law firms or powerful financial, governmental, or industrial institutions is staffed almost exclusively by graduates of Ivy League colleges, such impressions are much more myth than reality. All higher educational institutions are financially dependent on social philanthropy. Whether public funds are tax supported or private funds are tax exempted should logically have no bearing on qualities of higher educa tion in New England or elsewhere. But whether public and private institutions of higher education compete or cooperate in raising and using public and private funds will seriously affect qualities of New England higher education and its role in regional economic development during the 1980s.

Private and public colleges and universities should cooperate: by developing and staffing complementary instead of redundant curricula and programs; by scheduling courses and transporting students among different, neighboring institutions; by making equitable arrangements for sharing tuition income; and by pooling common resources for maintaining and supplying their operations. The Five Colleges consortium of Amherst, Smith, Mt. Holyoke, Hampshire Colleges, and the University of Massachusetts has established an effective precedent for such cooperation. The experiment could be adopted and expanded by private and public institutions throughout New England.

There are also competitive pressures among institutions offering different degrees in higher education. The issue is whether universities with undergraduate, postgraduate, and professional schools offer postsecondary education superior to those of community colleges offering only para-professional or associate degrees, or four-year colleges offering only baccalaureate degrees. Among academicians the emphasis has been in favor of advanced degree programs. So there have been pressures to establish postgraduate or specialized facilities and programs that are redundant, wasteful, and of questionable quality. Here again, higher education may do itself more harm than good if faculty and administrators, community colleges, four-year colleges and universities fail to cooperate in developing and staffing complementary, nonredundant curricula and programs.

A SINGLE INSTITUTE FOR REGIONAL DEVELOPMENT CONTRACT SERVICES

During 1945–75, because of Veterans' benefits, the Defense Education Act, and response to needs for more research in aerospace-defense, wealth and manpower devoted to higher education grew faster than ever before. As a result, academic freedom for more specialized, intellectual pursuits on and off campus has become more important than academic responsibilities for maintaining the integrity of the college or university as an institution or community of scholars. In the 1950s C. P. Snow lamented the split between the "Two Cultures," sciences and humanities, on campus;[10] and Jacques Barzun lamented the deteriorating human and cultural qualities of the "House of Intellect."[11] By the 1960s Clark Kerr used the term "multiversity" because the university had been transformed into a conglomerate of academic fiefdoms and administrative bureaucracies.[12]

As a result of this fragmentation, intellectual enlightenment seems to have been measured more by the number and variety of academic disciplines than by efforts to preserve either the collegiality of intellectual interests or the responsibilities for self-governance by faculty members, trustees, administrators, staff, and students. Moral enlightenment of the campus community or institutions at large has been taken too much for granted, hence neglected. Bureaucratic or technocratic special interests are dominant over common, general interests. The university now suffers from what Tom Wolfe has called the me generation.

On one campus twelve different departments offer courses or field research projects on urban and environmental quality problems. At the same university, faculty members of the Department of English have refused to teach grammar and composition, so a separate, less prestigious Department of Rhetoric and Composition has been established. At another university thirteen different departments offer courses in statistics, seven in financial accounting. Faculty and students of compartmentalized academic or professional disciplines develop their own lexicon about the rigorous qualities of their work. This compartmentalization makes it difficult to distinguish between intellectualism and specialized jargon about fundamental issues of society and governance.

Rather than a duty assumed by all members of the campus community, university development has become a term for the administrative function of fund-raising, presumably to finance the growth of existing disciplines or the proliferation of new disciplines. Faculty members used to participate in raising and budgeting funds; recruiting, admitting, counseling, and disciplining students; and relating to parents, alumni, and the public. Today these duties are affairs of administrative bureaucracies under the direction of vice presidents, vice chancellors, or deans. Those officers used to conduct regular classes for students, but their large staffs now demand and receive full-time attention. During recent years the growth of administrative staff has exceeded the growth of faculty; according to the National Education Association, for every hundred faculty members in colleges of the United States there are twenty-four administrators.[13]

Fragmentation of the university community into independent, special-interest groups has been accentuated by their complicity with counterpart special-interest bureaucracies of industry and government. We have already noted the agribusiness-government complex, the military-industrial complex, and the governmental and professional associations for health and medical services, associations of lawyers, computer scientists and manufacturers, econometricians, and the work of faculty members as part-time consultants or entrepreneurs in burgeoning markets of the "knowledge industry." As a result, collegiality and democratic self-governance have seen difficult times. Faculty senates exist, but they merely advise and rarely dissent from policies established by administrative bodies. Similarly, few students participate in governance; most, following examples set by faculty members, join special-interest groups that correspond to their purposes. As long as funds and programs were expanded or proliferated, faculty members, administrators, and students could concentrate on doing their own thing; there was no need to confront one another over the matter of sharing common goals or limited resources. Now, however, demographic and economic restrictions are forcing such confrontations and testing the strength of these relationships.

The gains of one group likely mean sacrifices by another, and these trade-offs strain bonds of trust and weaken the spirit of community. Such distrust may reflect a similar lack of confidence in industry and government to correct problems of inflation, energy, unemployment, crime, pollution, and so on. Most leaders of industry, government, and the professions were thoroughly indoctrinated during their college years with the notion of advancing specialized self-interests; they took for granted a democratic community of interests or abdicated to special bureaucracies responsibilities for the preservation of this community. In a large sense, therefore, the malaise in governance of university affairs may be a cause rather than a reflection of the malaise in affairs at large.

Some university officials, like their counterparts in business, blame government bureaucracy for its encroachment in affairs of higher education; and they may be justified in their complaint. But there is also a human and bureaucratic tendency to blame others for difficulties caused primarily by the failure of self-governance.

Yet, the climate of turbulence and necessity is also one of opportunity for the university to restore itself by helping other institutions. Archibald MacLeish once said, "A truly responsible university would... accept as the critical contemporary fact the failure of the balance between society and self and would find the reason for that failure in the dehumanizing of the culture on the one side and the dehumanizing of self on the other... It would commit itself to education as a vehicle for realization of self *in* society—and it would underline the 'in'."[14]

To realize itself *in* society the university should establish a community or regional services institute. Faculty members and students working on projects would participate in an educational experience as well as in formal academic study. Participants would provide research or advisory services for community improvements. The institute would be *the* facility through which the university would consolidate purposes of interdisciplinary research, teaching, regional services, and financial development.

If more trust is to develop between people and their institutions, both must learn more about their needs for interdependence and growth. Both must know more about the total set of facilities and organizations responsible for finance, education, housing, transportation, energy, employment, health, security, and safety environmental controls and recreation. The set must be complete and each subsystem must be compatible with all others from every standpoint: technical, financial, legal, political, aesthetic, and moral. To provide such knowledge the university should consolidate its existing centers, laboratories, clinics, and institutes that are now engaged independently in specialized field services into a single institute for community or regional development services. The institute would be conducted so that traditional, academic purposes of higher education (that is, enlightening students and freely pursuing knowledge for its own sake) would be sustained, and risks of conflicts of interests would be minimized. It would provide interdisciplinary, experiential education and research services with intellectual qualities compatible with those of traditional academic disciplines of education and research.

All professional staff members would, without exception, hold dual status as faculty members or as students identified with academic departments. Although not all academicians would be required to accept assignments in interdisciplinary projects of the institute, those who did so would be required to serve in teaching or research programs of academic departments. Fulltime assignments on institute projects could be limited to a maximum of two years. Policies requiring dual status and rotating staff would help to strengthen ties between academic and experiential-interdisciplinary aspects of higher education conducted on and off campus. They would also help to avoid the disadvantage of second-class citizenship conferred upon faculty and students working off campus on economic development projects (as has happened to university staff members on agricultural extension projects).

Faculty members who are already engaged independently as part-time staff members or consultants for client organizations would be encouraged, perhaps required, to work on projects of the institute solely on behalf of their university. Because faculty members would serve as educators of students while working on behalf of their university to provide services to client organizations, conflict of interest would be reduced.

Staff members of the institute would be compensated for their services in the same way that physicians, surgeons, and interns in the university's medical school are paid. The amount of compensation, although generally higher than for time devoted to academic programs, would depend on staff contributions to each project and on revenues derived from services rendered. The university could thus appropriate for itself the advantages of services and revenues that enterprising faculty members have acquired for themselves.

Fees would be charged for most services comparable with fees charged by other firms in the knowledge industry. These revenues would defray not only the direct costs of services but also the indirect costs of research and teaching activities more or less related to the work of the institute. Some might ask why such services should not be rendered without charge, in keeping with a tradition of free agricultural extension services of state-supported universities. The answer is that these services are intended not for farmers but for agribusinesses, which can afford to pay and should do so. If services were performed without fee, then privately financed research and consulting firms would be justified in complaints about unfairness of subsidized competition. By charging fees to organizations able and willing to pay and by conducting service projects as integral parts of its higher-education programs for student-interns, the university would avoid such complaints. Moreover, its clients would be more likely to appreciate and utilize its services *because* they paid fees.

Projects would be conducted under terms of legally binding contracts between the university and client organizations for regional development services genuinely needed and used by client-organizations. In each contract the university would retain rights of access and use for educational purposes of all information acquired or developed by faculty and students pursuant to their work. Political, bureaucratic, or proprietary interests of clients could be protected and confidential relations preserved by disguising or withholding the identity of clients and their interests. The university, however, would reserve rights to information, not just to avoid complicity with partisan political or private commercial interests but also to preserve its cardinal purposes of freedom in pursuing knowledge. If the client-organization could not agree to such provisions for information, the university should decline to sign the contract.

All projects would be staffed by faculty members and students working together. This arrangement would help correct the flaw of some internship programs in which the student is put in the awkward position of having to please two bosses with different interests—professors of the university who are responsible for their intellectual and professional development, and supervisors of client organizations who are responsible for results of their work assignments. Because the purpose of the projects is to educate students as well as to serve clients, the professor, not the staff members of the client organization, should be responsible for work assignments and performance evaluations of students. But executives of client organizations would assess the acceptability of the work of both professors and students acting as agents of their university. Thus students, not just faculty members, should derive benefits from field-project experiences. And executives of client organizations would evaluate and receive benefits of the work of universities. Gaps between academic theories and practical problems of community and regional development could be reduced. Moreover, most clients would require cooperative efforts of specialists in scientific, technical, financial, administrative, or humanistic aspects of the project. Such experiences would engender more cooperation and mutual respect among faculty and students concerned with academic problems on campus.

Before signing a binding contract for each project, the directorate of the institute would approve the purpose, plan, organization, proposed methods, and budget. This policy would assure that the work of each project is in accordance with the university's concept of higher education, thus helping to avoid pitfalls of commercialism or vocationalism and ensuring compatibility of academic education on campus and experiential education of regional development projects off campus.

As an example of this policy, Harvard University recently decided not to sponsor a genetic engineering company that would manufacture drugs and earn large revenues.[15] Under terms of the Patent and Trademark of 1980, however, Stanford University, which claims it develops a patentable idea every fourteen working hours, was reported to have earned $600,000, and MIT $700,000, by licensing private companies to use some of those ideas.[16]

The importance of the role of the president, trustees, and leaders of community or regional organizations in implementing this proposal cannot be overestimated. Consolidating already existing field activities of universities would require that they take strong initiatives. The campus is too compartmentalized for grass-roots initiatives of faculty or students to be effective. For example, strong resistance to consolidation would likely come from schools of medicine, public health, nursing, nutrition, biochemistry, and pharmacology whose faculty and administrators might prefer to protect their own turf and exercise their academic or professional license on their own terms, instead of on behalf of the university as a whole. But with active support of the president and trustees and with the cooperation of leaders of community or regional organizations, project by project the university could become an institutional activist in the community or region, and special-interest groups on campus would learn the advantages of interdisciplinary cooperation and governance of affairs on campus—all without threatening to interfere with those who pursue specialized academic work. The president and trustees would, of course, ensure that promotions, salary increases, or tenure were rewarded as liberally for contributions to economic development projects of the institute as for contributions to academic disciplines. They would also encourage leaders of community organizations to enter into contracts with the university. And community leaders would have to be willing to do business with the university, as they have with commerical research or consulting firms.

That the university can act as educator or honest broker for leaders of regional or community organizations to work together more effectively can be easily illustrated. A few years ago a small group of professors and students made a brief reconnaissance study of the financing, organization, and management of a program to clean up a river near their university. They met with officials of government, industry, and conservations groups in several towns and cities and soon discovered conflicts in their approaches to the program and almost no coordination of efforts. Before completing the project, they invited leaders of these communities to a meeting on campus. The professors and students ostensibly wanted to thank the community leaders for their cooperation and inform them of the results of the study, but the main purpose was to bring them together on neutral ground, so they might begin their own process of participatory management. The university group discussed its findings and offered suggestions for more effective ways to reconcile conflicting interests of business, government, and conservationists in cleaning up the river. As a result, community leaders decided to continue meeting together, and urged the university group to broaden its purposes and expand its staff to provide information about the clean-up program's effects on employment, land-use planning, pollution control, and taxes. Without the impetus provided by the university's invitation to meet, the leaders of these special-interest groups might not otherwise have been willing to work with one another on their common problems.

The university can serve as an activating catalyst of community or regional development processes that heretofore have floundered because of unresolved issues. For examples: questions of responsibility and authority of community, regional, state, or federal government, and of private organizations for mass transportation, management of land and water resources, health, and safety; also their financing operations, regulation, and improvements. It is at the community and regional levels that American industrial, governmental, and eleemosynary organizations together with the help of college or universities are likely to find new ways to serve society more effectively. The effectiveness of efforts emanating from Federal bureaucracies in Washington to managing processes for community and regional development has been a very controversial issue. Because the college or university is held in high esteem by all people, I believe that their efforts to participate *as institutions* in processes for regional economic and cultural development would be well received.

For the university to succeed in these efforts to restore itself by serving others, academic and administrative officers must subordinate their special interests to the university's purpose of moral and intellectual enlightenment of all. A major reason for problems of cultural and economic development in the United States is that leaders of our institutions have acted on the presumption that they serve their institutions or community best if they concentrate on their specialized academic or professional disciplines or functions. But community interests cannot be taken for granted or ignored if democratic freedoms and processes for self-governance are to prevail. I am convinced that by channeling the energies and idealism of our youth together with the intellectualism and wisdom of faculty, administrators, and trustees the college or university can, indeed, expand its role in regional economic development in the 1980s.

APPENDIX I
The Leadership Opinion Poll on Higher Education and the Economy

Melvin H. Bernstein and Irwin Harrison

I. INTRODUCTION

It is widely recognized that New England has a heavy concentration of some of the oldest and most highly regarded colleges and universities in the nation. The ideas and inventions generated by the campuses and their graduates are an underlying source of strength for the economic development of the region. However, higher education has not been traditionally thought of as an industry. If it is regarded as an industry now, what is its importance to the economy? Is it performing up to its capability? What can it contribute to the economy beyond what it is presently doing?

A survey was commissioned by the New England Board of Higher Education to find out what leaders of business, government, higher education, think-tank institutes, and the media think about the role of colleges and universities in fostering economic development. The survey was designed to elicit opinions from these leaders concerning the importance of higher education to development, whether they think much at all about higher education, and whether they perceive higher education as an industry. They were asked their opinions about the greatest opportunities for economic growth and stability in the region, their evaluation of colleges and universities in helping to meet labor-force needs of private industry, the extent of communication between institutions of higher learning and other sectors of the economy, and their ideas of how to improve communication if they feel it needs improvement.

It was assumed that though many leaders understood in a general way the importance of higher education to the health of the economy, they did not actively think about the relationship and the opportunities it presents for cooperation. The questions were designed to trigger the potential thinking of those who, once activated, would have important ideas to contribute.

Questionnaires were mailed to 1,200 New England leaders between late October and early December 1980. The 400 respondents included 133 from private industry, 160 from higher education, 97 from state government, five from labor, and five from the United States Congress. The response rate of 33 percent is considered satisfactory for a mail survey, particularly one that included several open-ended questions. The sources of the 400 responses were related geographically to the concentration of population in the six New England states. Sixty percent of the business leaders who responded were chief executive officers of their corporations, and 67 percent of the responding educators were presidents of their institutions. All six governors and most state legislative leaders responded to the survey. Sixty-three percent of respondents have lived in New England for at least twenty-five years. The findings reported below are related to major points discussed in the book.

II. FINDINGS OF KEY QUESTIONS

A. *Higher Education as an Industry*

"Do you or do you not think of New England's public and private institutions as an industry in the region's economy?"

Do think of as an industry	80%
Do not think of as an industry	20

B. *Role of Higher Education*

"Before today, how often, if at all, had you thought about what the role of New England's colleges and universities should be in helping New England achieve maximum growth and stability in the 1980s?"

Very often	39%
Fairly often	29
Occasionally	26
Just once or twice	4
Not at all	2

C. *Importance of Higher Education to the Economy*

"How important do you think New England's institutions of learning are to the economy of the region?"

Very important	79%
Fairly important	18
Not too important	3
Not important at all	0*
Do not really know	0*

*(less than .5 of 1%)

D. *Meeting Manpower Needs*

"How would you rank New England's colleges and universities on helping to meet the various labor-force needs of private industry in the region?"

Outstanding	13%
Above average	34
Average	35
Below average	16
Poor	2

E. Communications between Business and Higher Education
"Do you think there is or is not enough communication between New England's higher education institutions and the region's business community on how they can help each other?"

Enough communication	12%
Not enough communication	88

F. Communications between Government and Higher Education
"Do you think there is or is not enough communication between New England's higher education institutions and government in the region on how they can help each other?"

Enough communication	23%
Not enough communication	77

G. How to Improve Communications
"If you feel communication between New England's higher education institutions and private industry or government can be improved, please explain."

Increase cooperation between the state, business and education	51%
More interaction between education and business	37
Discuss mutual needs	12
Education should provide the manpower needed	9

H. Location in New England
"If you are in private industry, do you expect your firm to continue to be located in New England for the forseeable future or do you expect the firm to move out of the region?"

Expect to be located in New England for forseeable future	97%
Expect to move out of region	3

I. Economic Growth in New England
"What do you think the greatest opportunities are for economic growth and stability in New England in the 1980s?"

High technology industry	67%
Tourism/Recreation	25
Education	17
Energy development	14
Service industries	11
Manufacturing	11

J. Economic Growth in the States

"What do you think the greatest opportunities are for economic growth and stability in your state in the 1980s?"

High technology industry	64%
Tourism/Recreation	25
Education	16
Manufacturing	13
Energy development	12
Service industries	11

K. Role of Sectors of the Economy to Promote Growth

"What do you think the role of the sector of the economy you represent should be to help New England achieve maximum economic growth and stability in the 1980s?"

1. *Business*	
Improve business climate/attract more business	20%
Increase capital investment	20
Improve productivity	18
Provide jobs	15
2. *Higher Education*	
Provide a well-trained work force	42%
Expand technical education and training	26
Cooperation between business and education	25
Provide funds for research and development/innovative research and development	16
3. *State Government*	
Improve business climate/attract more business	41%
Tax reform	25
Expand technical education and training	17
Less government regulation/red tape	13

III. DISCUSSION OF FINDINGS

The survey results confirm the assumption that New England's colleges and universities have an important role to play in the economic life of the region. Eighty percent of the respondents thought that higher education is recognized as an industry. However, this view of higher education has become emphasized only in recent years, and because of growing economic problems. It can be argued that higher education as an industry has largely been invisible in the past. To achieve better public understanding of its economic significance, higher education will have to present its role as an industry more aggressively and more clearly.

That 68 percent of the region's leaders think "very often" or at least "fairly often" about how the colleges and universities can help achieve economic growth suggests the broad opportunity that is available for collaboration in this field. Whether the potential will be fulfilled is another question.

Again, the potential for fruitful cooperation is indicated by the 79 percent of leaders who view higher education as "very important" to the region's economy. Nevertheless, 88 percent of leaders find there is not enough communication between higher education and the business community, and 77 percent find communication between higher education and government insufficient. Open-ended responses to the question indicated that while there was not enough communication, the quality of communications was even more inadequate.

As to the problem of extent of interaction, a major newspaper publisher who found communication lacking said "more dialogue is needed between the sectors through forums and media coverage." On the issue of quality of communication, the chief executive officer of one of the largest corporations in New England noted, "I don't think the different elements have learned to speak in each other's language to an adequate degree."

When asked to explain how communications can be improved between higher education and private industry or government, 51 percent felt cooperation should be increased among the states, business, and education. However, an examination of the leadership subtotals reveals most business leaders, 53 percent, favored *direct* interaction between education and business to foster better communications. Sixty-two percent of educators and 63 percent of government leaders, on the other hand, emphasized a *tripartite* approach, including educators, business, and government, to improve communication. This difference in emphasis suggests a business distrust of government involvement which will require time and effort to overcome. Government leaders appear to recognize this need, since their number one priority as reported in the survey is in helping to produce economic growth and stability in the 1980s by improving the business climate of their states.

Recent national and regional economic pressures, compounded by the gap between supply and demand of skilled manpower, force unfavorable attention on higher education's role in meeting labor force needs of private industry. Only 47 percent of responding leaders ranked higher education "above average" or "outstanding" in meeting those needs, while 53 percent ranked the campuses as "average" or lower. In view of New England's intense competition with Sunbelt states for skilled manpower, particularly in the high technology growth industries, more attention is now being given to higher education's effectiveness in generating manpower supply.

IV. CONCLUSION

Overall, the survey shows that New England's leadership regards higher education as an important asset to the region—an asset that significantly influences future economic prospects. At the same time, the findings leave little doubt that a renewed collective effort is needed among leaders in business and higher education on the one hand, and government and higher education on the other, in order to engage academia effectively in contributing to the region's economy.

APPENDIX II
Perspectives of Two Business Leaders

RAY STATA, PRESIDENT, ANALOG DEVICES, INC. MASSACHUSETTS

Higher education faces an enormous challenge in the next decade. Financial resources are dwindling under the pressure of inflation, tax revolt, and fiscal crises, while demand for certain segments of education such as engineering is growing dramatically. The ability of higher education to reallocate resources is limited. Under these conditions we must look to new directions to meet the challenge. First, adult and continuing education will have to play an important role in relieving the short-term engineering supply crunch. There is a tremendous opportunity to retrain underutilized adult professionals for employment in the high-technology industry. For example, the Massachusetts High Technology Council together with the Massachusetts Teachers Association have put together a model program to retrain recently unemployed school teachers to become computer programmers. The first class graduated from a twenty-six week fulltime course last year. That program has been enormously successful both from the viewpoint of the individuals involved and the needs of industry. In many instances the financial resources to sustain this career transition have been obtained from federal government loans to the students. This suggests a model for federal government loan support, so that adult students bear the ultimate responsibility for the education cost of career transitions. As another example of adult education, the Council has also worked closely with Northeastern University to establish a master's degree program in engineering for women with science and math backgrounds who, because of family obligations or previous career directions, have not been prepared to participate in the high technology industry.

As a second point I would argue that industry will have to shoulder a larger responsibility in the financing of higher education, particularly in such growth sectors as engineering. Unless industry provides equipment and faculty support to finance the growth of engineering schools, graduates will just not be available in sufficient quantity to meet the needs of industry. Federal tax legislation can go a long way toward facilitating this financing mechanism. For example, the American Electronics Association has filed a bill in Congress to allow a tax deduction of the full selling price of equipment donated to universities and other educational institutions. This would provide a significant incentive to industry in comparison to the present circumstances, where they can only deduct from taxes the cost of the equipment so donated. Another approach would be for the federal government to provide matching grants for all monies donated by industry to higher education either directly or through tax relief.

As a final point, I would like to comment briefly on one other troublesome issue. That is, with the emphasis being given to engineering and scientific education because of economic imperatives, there is an understandable tendency for the interest of the humanist and the technologist to polarize. Both the technologist and the humanist must struggle hard to prevent this polarization. Along these lines I would make one observation: the better engineering schools have come a long way toward increasing the humanist content of their required engineering and scientific curricula. It is not clear that the humanists have gone nearly as far in increasing the scientific and engineering content of a liberal arts education. In view of the fact that an increasing number of liberal arts graduates will pursue professional careers in the high technology industry, it would seem appropriate that they be given more exposure to what computers, science, and engineering are all about, so that they will have a background and confidence to study these subjects further should their later career development take them in these directions. It is not necessary that the president and the general manager of a high technology company have an engineering or science degree, but it is necessary that they acquire a comfortable knowledge of the products and the technology that drive their particular business segment.

The goals of humanists and technologists, I believe, in time will move closer together as we all come to understand better the implications of modern society on the purpose and content of higher education. The education of technologists must increasingly prepare people to take on leadership roles in government, industry, education, and other institutions, where an appreciation of history and cultural values are so important. At the same time, the education of humanists must likewise prepare people to take on leadership roles in these same institutions at a time when science and engineering will play a more important role. In the last analysis, the purpose of education is to prepare people to cope with their journey through life, to live happy, productive lives, and to leave their mark in some small way on the progress of mankind. At this point in history, neither a strictly technological nor a strictly humanist education is adequate for this task.

RUSSELL BRACE, CHAIRMAN OF THE BOARD, DIVERSIFIED COMMUNICATIONS, INC. MAINE

Over the last few years in the state of Maine I have spent a disproportionate amount of time pleading for a higher level of cooperation between the public sector, as represented by government, and private industry. It has been my feeling that economic development, job creation, gross state product, state industry attraction, value-added products, and existing business growth cannot be accomplished unless the public sector and the private sector create and run a corporation for this very purpose.

Related to economic innovation, job creation, and encouragement of the growth of small business was the great need for creation of a capital corporation to encourage capital formation and capital investment. It culminated in an act of the legislature two years ago which created the Maine Development Foundation, a quasi-public concern that is funded both by the state legislature and by equal funds from the private sector. In the same session of the legislature, the Maine Capital Corporation was created, giving investors special tax considerations for investment in this company, which now holds a license from the SBA as an SBIC.

The next phase of my interest will be to work for a special linkage now between public, private, and educational institutions and to suggest ways and styles that colleges and universities could use to come closer to economic development in Maine.

It has been said that scientists have discovered so many substitutes these days that it is hard to remember what is truly original. Well, there has been no substitute for the entrepreneur who truly represents innovation—a vital ingredient in the nation's economic growth and rising standard of living. Unfortunately, the entrepreneur has been besieged to the point where there is a distinct fall-off of innovative activity. Causes include mounting government regulations, negative impact of inflation on profitability, a higher exposure to failure, and, indeed, longer payback periods of untried or new products.

Although scientists cannot and will not invent a substitute for entrepreneurs, I feel the time has come when this segment of the business community needs some assistance from the vast resources of our colleges and universities. Traditionally, assistance has been sought from the government. Yet enormous untapped sources happen to exist within the vast educational community of America.

We cannot forget for a minute that most of the funding of higher education in our society is contributed by the private sector. We should not forget that small business represents the backbone of any state's economy. In New England 86 percent of separate businesses have fewer than twenty employees, while 94 percent have fewer than 100. These are dramatic numbers, and unless public, private, and educational institutions work together, we may see a paralysis in the backbone.

I mentioned earlier how the state legislature in Maine funded the creation of the Maine Development Foundation with matching funds to be provided by the private sector. The plan is very successful, although it is only two years old. I also mentioned that the Maine Capital Corporation provides certain tax considerations for those who bought shares in this capital company. I would like to present a few ideas as to how we can bring educational institutions closer to the private sector and I know, as the survey in Appendix I has shown, that there is not enough communication between New England higher education institutions and the business community on how the two can work hand in glove.

One way is certainly for the colleges and universities to provide people or a labor force, well trained in specific areas. Private industry looks to colleges and universities to do this job, and some institutions do it better than others. I suggest that colleges and universities invite members of the private sectors to discuss and even establish requirements and standards which they wish applied to student preparation for specialized fields.

Second, corporations need to be willing to underwrite the cost of publishing important studies by specialists at the universities. Too often we see studies that are completed, read by others in the same department, put on the shelf, and left to collect dust. And no one can forget that some of the great papers that have been published have been financed by the private sector.

Third, I have encouraged the private sector to make greater use of our educators on boards of directors. It has been my pleasure to serve on several boards with educators; whether they were technically oriented, economists, or administrative specialists, these individuals have contributed to the success of the corporation they are directing, and provide a special perspective welcomed by those who are usually called from the business community.

Fourth, I would encourage private industry, working closely with a college or university, to take an inventory of the people resources that are available within an institution and the means of getting access. How often I hear that the small businessman or entrepreneur does not know how to get additional information or how to evaluate a certain product by using the resources of a university.

Fifth, colleges and universities should be invited to participate with statewide industry trade associations that emphasize new products and new product testing and marketing. The spillover effect here is to tell the private sector that a college and university does have an understanding of entrepreneurship and the realities of the free enterprise system. Too often, I believe, there is a "we-they" syndrome, each not knowing or sometimes not even trusting the motivations of the other.

Sixth, colleges and universities should consider the creation of venture capital corporations, using their own resources. Such a corporation should be a subsidiary of their board of trustees. We all know that this has happened in certain of the larger colleges and universities, and such a broadened trend would greatly benefit both business and higher education in New England. I would encourage members of the private sector to sit on the board of the venture capital company and the university venture capital corporation to use highly trained businessmen to run it. An article by Seymour and Wetzel in the *New England Journal of Business and Economics* in the spring of 1980 supports the thesis that this region must do more to stimulate economic development. The authors came to the following conclusions in an article entitled "An Economic Strategy for New England" (page 400):

One. New England depends on smaller manufacturing firms for a larger portion of its employment than the U.S. as a whole.

Two. New England's competitive economic advantages include a skilled, stable, and relatively low paid labor force, a reservoir of technical know-how, a substantial pool of professional venture capital, and a tradition of Yankee entrepreneurship.

Three. In recent years, New England has not combined these resources to spawn new ventures fast enough to replace ventures that have disappeared or moved elsewhere.

I believe strongly that these findings indicate the necessity of moving swiftly to link business and higher education in mutually profitable ventures.

NOTES

I. EMERGING NEEDS OF A REINDUSTRIALIZED ECONOMY

1. *New York Times* (October 20, 1980).

2. Estall, *New England: A Study in Industrial Adjustment* (New York: Frederick A. Praeger, 1966).

3. *Time* (September 1, 1980).

4. *Manchester Union Leader* (October 21, 1980).

5. *The New England Economy: A Report to the President* (Washington, D.C.: U.S. Government Printing Office, 1951).

6. Harris, *The Economics of New England: Case Study of an Older Area* (Cambridge, Mass.: Harvard University Press, 1952).

7. The results of the survey can be found in *Issues* (Wenham, Mass.: New England Board of Higher Education, March 1981). The comments quoted here and elsewhere in the introductory chapter have not been published before. The sources of these comments are treated confidentially as provided in the survey.

8. Ibid.

9. Unpublished remark made as panel moderator, Hartford, Connecticut, conference of the Commission on Higher Education and the Economy, Hartford Insurance Group Tower, December 16, 1981.

10. *New High Technology Recruitment Index* (New York: Deutsch, Shea and Evans, 1979).

11. *Engineering and High Technlology Manpower Shortages: The Connection with Mathematics* (Atlanta, Georgia: Southern Regional Conference Board, 1980).

12. Unpublished comments, leadership survey of New England Board of Higher Education (Wenham, Mass.: December 1980).

13. Conference of State Manufacturers' Associations, *Manufacturing Business Climates of the Forty-Eight Contiguous States of America* (Chicago, Ill.: Alexander Grant, 1980).

14. *Issues* (above, n. 7).

II. AN ECONOMIC CONTEXT FOR HIGHER EDUCATION

1. *Prospectus for the Commission on Higher Education and the Economy of New England* (Wenham, Mass.: New England Board of Higher Education, December 16, 1980).

2. Fred E. Crossland, "Learning to Cope with Downward Slope," remarks delivered at the annual meeting of the Association of Independent Colleges and Universities in Massachusetts, Worcester, May 8, 1980.

3. *World Almanac and Book of Facts: 1981* (New York: 1980).

4. Lynn E. Browne, "Remarks before the New England Economic Project" (Boston: June 27, 1980).

5. Robert W. Eisenmenger, *The Dynamics of Growth in New England's Economy: 1870–1964* (Middletown, Conn.: Wesleyan University Press, 1967).

6. "The New England Regional Plan: An Economic Development Strategy," draft (Boston: New England Regional Commission, September 15, 1980).

7. Browne (above, n. 4).

8. U.S. Department of Labor, Bureau of Labor Statistics, *Projections of Industrial Employment in New England to 1985* (Boston: New England Regional Office, 1977).

III. MARKET INFLUENCES ON HIGHER EDUCATION

1. See Edward Denison, *Accounting for Slower Economic Growth* (Washington, D.C.: The Brookings Institution, 1979).

2. See, for example, Theodore W. Schultz, "Investment in Human Capital," *American Economic Review*, Vol. 51 (1961), 1–17. Gary Becker, *Human Capital: A Theoretical and Empirical Analysis with Special Reference to Education* (New York: Columbia University Press, for the National Bureau of Economic Research, 1964). Jacob Mincer, "The Distribution of Labor Income: A Survey with Special References to the Human Capital Approach," *Journal of Economic Literature*, Vol. VIII (1970), 1–26.

3. Denison, *op. cit.*

4. Samuel Bowles and Hubert Gintis, *Schooling in Capitalist America* (New York: Basic Books, 1976).

5. Carnegie Commission on Higher Education, *Reform on Campus* (New York: McGraw-Hill, 1972).

6. See Richard B. Freeman, *The Overeducated American* (New York: Academic Press, 1976).

7. See Denison, *op. cit.;* and Zvi Griliches, "Returns to Research and Development in the Private Sector," in John W. Kendrick and Beatrice N. Vaccara, eds., *New Developments in Productivity Measurement and Analysis* (Chicago: University of Chicago Press, 1980), pp. 419–454. The view that the slowdown in R & D is a major explanation for the slowdown in productivity growth comes chiefly from John Kendrick. See, for example, Kendrick and Elliot S. Grossman, *Productivity in the United States* (Baltimore: The Johns Hopkins University Press, 1980). For a similar view see M. Ishag Nadiri, "Sectoral Productivity Slowdown," *American Economic Review*, Vol. 70 (1980), 349–352.

8. New England Regional Commission, "The New England Regional Plan: An Economic Development Strategy," draft (Boston, Mass.: New England Regional Commission, September 15, 1980).

9. Richard B. Freeman, *The Market for College-Trained Manpower* (Cambridge: Harvard University Press, 1971). Walter Fogel and Daniel Mitchell, "Higher Education Decision-Making and the Labor Market," in *Higher Education and the Labor Market*, ed. Margaret S. Gordon (New York: McGraw Hill, 1974). Bruce Wilkinson, "Present Values of Lifetime Earnings for Different Occupations," *Journal of Political Economy*, 74 (1966), 556–572. Richard E. Peter-

son, *American College and University Enrollment Trends in 1971* (Berkeley, Calif.: Carnegie Commission on Higher Education, 1972).

10. Neal R. Peirce, *The New England States* (New York: W. W. Norton, 1976), pp. 96–97. National Center for Education Statistics, *Projections of Educational Statistics to 1986–87* (Washington, D.C.: U.S. Government Printing Office, 1978), pp. 42–48.

11. *Projections of Educational Statistics to 1986–87*, pp. 44–48.

12. Nancy B. Doarman and Valena W. Plisko, National Center for Education Statistics, *The Condition of Education* (Washington, D.C.: U.S. Government Printing Office, 1980), p. 30.

13. Andrew J. Pepin for the National Center for Education Statistics, *Fall Enrollment in Higher Education 1978* (Washington, D.C.: U.S. Government Printing Office, 1979), pp. 190–191.

14. *Projections of Educational Statistics to 1986–87*, pp. 42–43.

15. Ibid., pp. 42–48.

16. U.S. Department of Commerce, *Census of the Population, 1960,* U.S. Summary, Tables 126, 127, pp. 272–277. *Census of the Population, 1970*, U.S. Summary, Table 165. pp. 506–509.

17. Leonard A. Lecht, *Changes in Occupational Characteristics: Planning Ahead for the 1980's* (New York: The Conference Board, 1976), appendix B.

18. Bernard Wysocki, Jr., "More Firms Avoid Hiring M.B.A.'s Due to High Pay, Other Problems," *Wall Street Journal*, September 12, 1980, p. 23.

19. U.S. Department of Commerce, *Census of the Population, 1960,* U.S. Summary, Tables 126, 127, pp. 272–277. *Census of the Population, 1970,* U.S. Summary, Table 165, pp. 506–509.

20. *Projections of Educational Statistics to 1986–87*, pp. 42–48.

21. Although a nationwide shortage of registered nurses exists, in many large metropolitan areas like Boston shortages are apparent only in some specialty areas. See U.S. Department of Labor, Bureau of Labor Statistics, *Employment Outlook for 1980 College Graduates in New England* (Boston: New England Regional Office, 1980), p. 10.

22. U.S. Department of Labor, Bureau of Labor Statistics, *Occupational Projections and Training Data* (Washington, D.C.: U.S. Government Printing Office, 1979), p. 70.

23. *CPC Salary Survey: A Study of Beginning Offers* (Bethlehem, Pa.: College Placement Council, 1973–1980). See also *Salary Survey of Supervisory and Nonsupervisory Professional Engineers* (Palo Alto, Calif.: American Electronics Association, annual).

24. Lecht, *Changes in Occupational Charateristics*, Appendix B.

25. National Center for Education Statistics, *Digest of Education Statistics 1963* (Washington, D.C.: U.S. Government Printing Office, 1963), p. 57. W. Vance Grant and Leo J. Eiden, for the National Center for Education Statistics, *Digest of Education Statistics 1980* (Washington, D.C.: U.S. Government Printing Office, 1980), p. 83.

26. *Digest of Education Statistics, 1980*, p. 119. *The Condition of Education, 1980*, p. 6.

27. *Facts about New England Colleges, Universities, and Institutes* (Wellesley, Mass.: New England Board of Higher Education, 1959, 1979).

28. *Digest of Education Statistics 1980*, pp. 115–117. National Center for Education Statistics, *Education Directory: Colleges and Universities* (Washington, D.C.: U.S. Government Printing Office, annual, 1968–1978).

29. *Education Directory: Colleges and Universities*, Annual, 1968–1978.

30. John A. Centra, *College Enrollment in the 1980's: Projections and Possibilities* (Princeton, N.J.: College Entrance Examination Board, 1978).

31. Centra, ibid., summarizes these studies, including those by Joseph Froomkin, *Changing Credential Objectives of Students in Post-Secondary Education* (Washington, D.C.: U.S. Government Printing Office, 1974) (middle projection); Allan Cartter, *Ph.D.'s and the Academic Labor Market* (New York: McGraw-Hill, 1976); Martin M. Frankel and Forrest W. Harrison, for the National Center for Education Statistics, *Projections of Educational Statistics to 1985–86* (Washington, D.C.: U.S. Government Printing Office, 1977) (low projection); Stephen P. Dresch, "Demography, Technology and Higher Education: Toward a Formal Model of Educational Adaptation," *Journal of Political Economy*, 83 (1975), 535–569. See also Richard B. Freeman, *The Declining Economic Value of Higher Education and the American Social System* (New York: Aspen Institute for Humanistic Studies Program in Education for a Changing Society, 1976); Fred E. Crossland, "Learning to Cope with a Downward Slope," *Change* (July/August 1980), 187.

32. Centra, *College Enrollment in the 1980's*, summarizes these studies, including those by Carnegie Foundation for the Advancement of Teaching, *More than Survival: Prospects for Higher Education in a Period of Uncertainty* (San Francisco: Jossey-Bass, 1975); Howard R. Bowen, "Higher Education: A Growth Industry?" *Educational Record*, 55, No. 3 (1974), 147–158; Larry L. Leslie and Howard F. Miller, Jr., *Higher Education and the Steady State*, ERIC/Higher Education Research Report, 4 (Washington, D.C.: American Association for Higher Education, 1974). See also Carol Frances, *College Enrollment Trends: Testing the Conventional Wisdom against the Facts* (Washington, D.C.: American Council on Education, 1980).

33. Centra, *College Enrollment in the 1980's*, summarizes these studies, including those by Carnegie Foundation, *More than Survival* (above note); J. Froomkin, *Recent Developments in Post-Secondary Education, 1970–75* (Washington, D.C.: Joseph Froomkin, Inc., 1976); Michael S. McPherson, "The Demand for Higher Education," in David W. Breneman and Chester E. Finn, Jr., eds., *Public Policy and Private Higher Education* (Washington, D.C.: Brookings Institution, 1978); John R. Minter and H. R. Bowen, *Private Higher Education: Annual Report on Financial and Education Trends in the Private Sector of American Higher Education* (Washington, D.C.: Association of American Colleges, 1977, 1978); Richard R. Spies, *The Effect of Rising Cost on College Choice* (New York: College Entrance Examination Board, 1973, 1978); and Humphrey Doermann, *The Future Market in College Admissions* (New York: College Entrance Examination Board, 1976). See also, F. E. Crossland, "Learning to Cope with a Downward Slope" (above, n. 31); National Center for Education Statistics, "Enrollment Declines Foreseen for Colleges in the 1980's" (Washington,

D.C.: U.S. Department of Health, Education, and Welfare, March 19, 1980), early release.

34. See Denison (above, n. 1).

35. For example, Jora Minasian, "Research and Development, Production Functions, and Rates of Return," *American Economic Review*, 59 (1969), 80–85 and N. Terleckyj, *Effects of R & D on the Productivity Growth of Industries: An Exploratory Study* (Washington, D.C.: National Planning Association, 1974).

36. Griliches (above, n. 7), and E. Mansfield, "Basic Research and Productivity Increase in Manufacturing," *American Economic Review*, (1980), 863–873.

37. See Kendrick and Grossman (above, n. 7), and Nadiri (above, n. 7).

38. Z. Griliches, "R & D and the Productivity Slowdown," *American Economic Review*, 70 (1980), 343–348.

39. See, for example, Gene Bylinsky, *The Innovation Millionaires* (New York: Charles Scribner's Sons, 1976), esp. Chapter 4, "Boston, the Cradle of Innovation."

40. Everett M. Rogers, John D. Eveland, and Alden S. Beon, *Extending the Agricultural Extension Model* (Stanford, Calif.: Institute for Communication Research, Stanford University, September 1976).

41. See Edward B. Roberts and Herbert A. Wainer: "New Enterprises on Route 128," *Science Journal* (December 1968); H.A. Wainer, "The Spin-Off of Technology from Government-Sponsored Research Laboratories: Lincoln Laboratory," unpublished M.S. thesis, M.I.T., Sloan School of Management, 1965; and Dan A. Forseth: "The Role of Government-Sponsored Research Laboratories in the Generation of New Enterprises—A Comparative Analysis," unpublished M.S. thesis, M.I.T., Sloan School of Management, 1966.

42. See Paul V. Teplitz, "Spin-Off Enterprises from a Large Government Sponsored Laboratory," unpublished M.S. thesis, M.I.T., Sloan School of Management, 1965.

IV. COMMUNITY ECONOMIC DEVELOPMENT

1. Schneider, *On the Nature of Cities* (San Francisco, Jossey-Bass, 1979).

2. Rowland, "In Hard Times, Colleges Need Good Neighbors," *Chronicle of Higher Education*, September 29, 1980.

3. Quoted in *New York Times*, February 4, 1976.

V. INITIATIVES TO ASSIST THE ECONOMY

1. Gross Domestic Product (GDP), unlike Gross National Product (GNP), excludes net income from abroad. As a result, GNP attributes output to the nation in which the producer resides while GDP attributes output to the nation where it originates. For the U.S. GDP for 1978 was 2,107.0 billion dollars; GNP was 2,127.1 billion dollars. In comparing the New England states with the U.S. as a whole, we have used the domestic product of each state or the gross state product. For further discussion see Lynn E. Browne and John S. Strong, "New England—13th Largest Country," *New England Economic Indicators* (July 1980), pp. A3, A4; Grace On, "Gross State Product in the New England States," ibid. (April 1980), pp. A4, A5; John H. Kendrick and C. Milton Jaycox, "The

Concept and Estimation of Gross State Product," *Southern Economic Journal*, 32, No. 2 (1965), 153–168.

2. Executive Office of the President, Office of Management and Budget, *Standard Industrial Classification Manual* (Washington, D.C.: U.S. Government Printing Office, 1972).

3. See, for example, Robert W. Eisenmenger, *The Dynamics of Growth in New England's Economy, 1870–1964* (Middletown: Wesleyan University Press, 1967); New England Regional Commission, *Report of the Task Force on Capital and Labor Markets* (Boston: New England Regional Economic Commission, November 12, 1975); New England Economic Advisory Committee to the New England Regional Commission, *The New England Regional Plan: An Economic Development Strategy–A Draft Proposal* (Boston: New England Regional Economic Commission, September 15, 1980); Price Waterhouse and Co., *New England Business: Profile and Analysis* (Boston: Price Waterhouse, September 30, 1976); J. S. Hekman, "What Attracts Industry to New England?" *New England Economic Indicators* (December 1978), pp. A3–A5.

4. Lynn E. Browne, "How Different Are Regional Wages?" *New England Economic Review*, (1978), 33–43. It is the adjustment for cost of living in New England that causes regional earnings to fall below the South Atlantic states and the East South Central states.

5. New England Economic Advisory Committee, pp. 16–17.

6. Ibid., pp. 37–38. Craig R. Seymour and William E. Wetzel, Jr., "An Economic Strategy for New England: The Role of Informal Equity Capital," *New England Journal of Business and Economics*, 6, No. 2 (1980), 1–12.

7. New England Economic Advisory Committee, pp. 1–6. For a discussion of regional changes in income differentials, see Lynn Browne, "Narrowing Regional Income Differentials," *New England Economic Review* (September/October 1980), 35–56.

8. Ibid., p. 17.

9. U.S. Department of Education, National Center for Education Statistics, *1980 Digest of Education Statistics* (Washington, D.C.: U.S. Government Printing Office), p. 155. In the District of Columbia, expenditures on private higher education for 1977–78 represented over 90 percent of total expenditures.

10. National Center for Education Statistics, *The Condition of Education, 1980* (Washington, D.C.: U.S. Government Printing Office), pp. 154–55.

11. Ibid.

12. Ibid.

13. For a more complete analysis employing data for the fiscal year 1976, see The National Institute of Education, *Higher Education Financing in Fifty States: Interstate Comparison, Fiscal Year 1976* (Washington, D.C.: U.S. Government Printing Office, 1979).

14. John S. Hekman, "New England's High Technology Industry is Here to Stay," *New England Economic Indicators* (March 1980), p. A5.

15. Ibid., p. A5. Hekman, "What Attracts Industry to New England?" *New England Economic Indicators* (December 1978), pp. A3–A5.

16. Ibid., p. A3.

17. Ibid., p. A4. See also Hekman, "The Future of High Technology Industry

in New England: A Case Study of Computers," *New England Economic Review*, (January/February 1980), 5–17; John S. Hekman, "Can New England Hold Onto Its High Technology Industry?" *New England Economic Review*, (March/April 1980), 35–44.

18. Richard F. Syron, A Changing New England," *New England Economic Indicators* (January 1979), pp. A3–A5.

19. Ibid., p. A5.

VI. NEW ENGLAND'S RESILIENCE

1. Tom Redburn, "New England's Rebirth a High-Technology Feat," *Los Angeles Times* (October 9, 1980).

2. *High School Graduates: Projections for the Fifty States*, joint publication of The Western Interstate Commission for Higher Education, National Institute of Independent Colleges and Universities, and Teachers Insurance and Annuity Assn., Boulder, Colo., November 1979.

3. Quoted in Redburn, note 1.

4. Ellis Katz, "The States Rediscovered Education in the 1970's," *State Government* (Winter, 1980), pp. 31ff.

5. Leonard P. Stavisky, "Education Policy and the Legislature: A Legislator's Overview," *State Legislatures* (September 1980), pp. 5ff.

6. Rochelle L. Stanfield, see "Campuses and Corporations: Industry Offers Money, but Not without Strings," *National Journal* (November 29, 1980), pp. 2021ff.

VII. EXPANDING ROLE IN N.E. ECONOMIC DEVELOPMENT

1. *Book of the States, 1980* (Council of State Governments, Lexington, Kentucky, 1979).

2. Howard Husock, "Boston: The In Place for College Students," *New York Times Magazine*, June 1, 1980, Section 6, pp. 22ff.

3. Higher Education General Information Survey (HEGIS), 1979, Massachusetts Board of Higher Education, 31 St. James Ave., Boston, Mass.

4. Address by Mary Newman, member of the Board of the Massachusetts Taxpayers' Foundation, and Professor, University of Massachusetts, Boston, cited in her address to the Third Invitational Seminar on Critical Issues in Higher Education in Massachusetts, Clark University, Worcester, Mass., May 29, 1980.

5. Estimated using data from the Higher Education General Information survey of total enrollments and average costs per resident student in the four-year public and private college or university.

6. "Market Value of Investments at 147 Colleges and Universities," compiled by the National Association of College and University Business Offices and published in the *Chronicle of Higher Education*, Washington, D.C., March 24, 1980.

7. "Artsachusetts," a public service advertisement, *Boston Globe*, Sunday, April 20, 1980.

8. *High School Graduates: Projections for the Fifty States*, Western Interstate Commission for Higher Education, Boulder, Colo., November 1979.

9. Muriel Cohen, "Applications on Rise at Most New England Colleges," *Boston Globe* (March 30, 1980), p. 39.

10. C. P. Snow, *The Two Cultures* (New York: Cambridge University Press, 1961).

11. Jacques Barzun, *The House of Intellect* (New York: Harper, 1959).

12. Clark Kerr, *The Uses of the University*, Godkin Lectures, Harvard University, 1963, (New York: Harper and Row, 1963).

13. W. S. Graybeal, "Ratios of Administrators to Teachers in Public Schools and Higher Educational Institutions, 1976–77," Report to the 56th NEA Representative Assembly, Washington, D.C., National Education Association, 1977.

14. Archibald MacLeish, address given at Hampshire College, October 1970. Excerpted under the title "Trustees of the Culture," *Saturday Review* (December 19, 1970), pp. 18–19.

15. Harvard's consideration and rejection of commercial possibilities of DNA research were reported in the *New York Times* (October 27, 1980), p. 1, (November 18, 1980), p. 1.

16. Timothy Aeppel, "Speeding Good Ideas from College to Marketplace," *Christian Science Monitor* (November 25, 1980), p. 2.

BIOGRAPHIES

Bernstein, Melvin H.

Director of Policy Studies, New England Board of Higher Education. Author of *The Prospectus* for the Commission on Higher Education and the Economy of New England (1980), and editor of *The Effective President* (1976).

Brace, Russell W.

Chairman, Diversified Communications, Inc. and New England Investment Group. Trustee, Nasson College and Director, Maine Development Foundation.

Curran, Ward S.

Professor and Chairman, Department of Economics, Trinity College. Author of *An Economic Approach to the Regulation of the Corporate Securities Markets* (1976) and *Principles of Financial Management* (1970).

Doeringer, Peter B.

Professor of Economics and Director, Institute on Employment Policy, Boston University. Editor, *Industrial Relations Research in International Perspective* (1981) and author, *Internal Labor Markets and Manpower Analysis* (1971).

Harrison, Irwin

President, Research/Analysis Corporation. Pollster for the *Boston Globe*.

Hoy, John C.

President, New England Board of Higher Education. Editor, *The Effective President* (1976) and author of *Choosing a College* (1967).

McGarrah, Robert E.

Professor of Management, University of Massachusetts at Amherst. Author, *Productivity Management: Text and Cases* (forthcoming 1981) and *Production and Logistics Management* (1963).

Pannell, Patricia F.

Assistant Professor of Economics, Bentley College and Research Associate, Institute for Employment Policy, Boston University.

Peirce, Neal R.

Contributing Editor, *The National Journal*. Author, *Economic Development: The Challenge of the 1980's* (1979) and *The New England States: People, Politics and Power in the Six New England States* (1976).

Stata, Ray

Chairman of the Board and President, Analog Devices, Inc. Member, Massachusetts Board of Regents; Chairman, Human Resource Development Committee of the Massachusetts High Technology Council.

Stokes, Charles J.

Charles Anderson Dana Professor of Economics, University of Bridgeport. Author, *Economics for Managers* (1979) and *Corporate Capital Budgeting* (1981).

Tandon, Pankaj

Assistant Professor of Economics, Boston University.

LIBRARY OF CONGRESS CATALOGING IN PUBLICATION DATA
Main entry under title:

Business and academia.

(A Futures of New England book)
Includes bibliographical references.
1. New England—Economic conditions—Addresses, essays, lectures. 2. Economic development—Effect of education on—Addresses, essays, lectures.
I. Hoy, John C. II. Bernstein, Melvin Herbert, 1914– III. New England Board of Higher Education. IV. Series.
HC107.A11B87 330.974'043 81-15940
ISBN 0-87451-197-6 AACR2